Golden Harvest

Reflections on rural team ministry for the fiftieth anniversary of the Hempnall Group of Parishes

Foreword by Graham James
Bishop of Norwich

Editors: Jill Turner and Sarah Patey

First published in 2013 by
The Hempnall Team Council
The Rectory
The Street
Hempnall
Norfolk
NR15 2AD

British Library Cataloguing-in-Publication Data
A catalogue record for this book is available from the British Library

ISBN 978-0-9545274-1-9

Printed in Great Britain by
The Lavenham Press, Lavenham, Suffolk CO10 9RN

Contents

Foreword

In this book Peter Moss comments that the Hempnall Group is exceptional since it has had unchanged boundaries for fifty years. While it isn't unique, it is certainly unusual over that course of time. I think one of the reasons there has been no change is that the parishes in the Hempnall Group have rather liked being with each other. This book, a successor to the one produced for the fortieth anniversary, is testimony to that. There is something significant to celebrate, a history for which gratitude is due.

The essays here mainly reflect on the recent past. A good number are written by clergy. So there is quite a lot about the value of a clergy team. There is also a good deal about the need for the lay people in a group of parishes to work as a team too. We take these things for granted in the contemporary church, forgetting how novel such ideas were only fifty years ago. They were a rediscovery of such a consistent theme in the New Testament that you wonder why Christians missed it for so long.

The very first thing Jesus did in his public ministry was to draw a group of disciples around him. He didn't exercise ministry on his own. The disciples are rather typical of the average parochial church council. There is an inner core (Peter, James and John) who get mentioned more than anyone else and seem to be the leaders, the churchwardens if you like. There are others with particular gifts. Andrew is always bringing people to Jesus. He is the evangelist with an eye for those outside. And then there are disciples such as Bartholomew or Thaddaeus, about whom we know nothing apart from their names. They may have done great work but they were the quiet ones. As well as the Twelve Jesus also sent out seventy people in pairs. Not on their own, you notice. There was a larger group of followers, not part of the group council or the parochial church council but whose mission was in the context of everyday life. Later, when the life of the Church got going, St Paul often speaks of his partnership in the gospel with fellow workers such as Titus, Timothy or Barnabas. Just in case this all sounds too cosy, let's remember Paul and Barnabas fell out over the qualities of another co-worker, John Mark. They went their separate ways. Some pastoral reorganisation was necessary because they couldn't work together.

The Hempnall Group will have had its ups and downs over fifty years. That's inevitable. But what I admire is the resolution of successive generations of clergy and lay people to work with each other in the service of the gospel. Such gospel work is also done for the common good and to the benefit of the communities within the group.

The ecclesiastical structures may not have changed over fifty years but the culture in which we now live and work is vastly different from the early 1960s. When the Group began the 'permissive society' had hardly begun. Philip Larkin thought it began 'between the end of the Chatterley ban and the Beatles' first LP'. That locates it in 1963. The sociologist of religion Callum Brown says the decline of the Church in Western Europe coincides with changes which happened in the 1960s, including the new freedom which women possessed as a result of the contraceptive pill. He contends it was women rather than the clergy who passed on the faith from generation to generation. He believes there was a major dislocation which began roughly at the time this Group was created. Mass membership organisations involving strong and regular commitment have also declined. By comparison with the early 1960s political parties in the United Kingdom and trade unions have suffered a much more catastrophic decline in membership than the Christian Church. But we know how the culture has changed, vividly illustrated in the way in which Sunday is now a day for sport, leisure activities and shopping rather than a day of rest and worship.

The rapidity of change means that some look upon rural communities romantically as places where the rhythms of a previous age are maintained. There is a belief that community life is stronger in our villages than in the city or our market towns. It isn't always so. But where it is stronger it is noticeable that the church is often at the heart of it. It may not be the case that a large number worship week by week, but our parish churches do not exist for themselves but for the communities they serve. Whenever I meet someone living in a Norfolk village they often know the name of their vicar or rector, even if he or she does not know them. That is rarely true of those who live in our towns or the City of Norwich. And why is it true? Because they have seen the vicar or rector (it does not matter whether it is someone who is stipendiary or non-stipendiary, they are always the vicar or rector) conduct a funeral or lead a carol service. The anonymity of life in the city means that attendances at some urban churches actually go down at Christmas. That is rarely true in the countryside. The boundaries between church and wider parish remain more blurred in our villages. Often it is the parish church which gives the village its sense of identity as the most significant building within it.

I am grateful for this record of service to God, the Church and the parishes of the Hempnall Group. It shines through the stories and testimonies here. It is a continuing story within a changed and challenging culture. Whatever the future holds for the Hempnall Group I am sure a sense of lay people and clergy working together for the sake of the gospel and in partnership with each other will be the hallmarks of mission and ministry in this place.

My prayers are with you as you celebrate fifty years of dynamic Group life proclaiming Jesus Christ in worship, prayer and service.

+Graham Norvic:

The Right Reverend Graham James, Lord Bishop of Norwich

September 2012

Acknowledgements

We thank all who have given so generously of their time to take part in this enterprise.

In particular, we have been overwhelmed by the willingness of all the clergy to give us their thoughtful responses to our initial invitation to reflect on their ministry before, during and after their time in the Group. They have given us much more than we could possibly have asked for. And we are delighted that Enid Gray and George Levack have so skilfully encapsulated their experience, as lay people, of worshipping in these villages.

We are most grateful to Graham James, Bishop of Norwich, for his insightful extended Foreword, and for his continuing support for this Group.

We thank members of the Team Council of the Hempnall Group for their encouragement and for entrusting this undertaking to us.

We are grateful to Monica Churchill for allowing us to use her line drawings, and to David Ferré for his photographic skill.

Finally, none of this would have happened without the encouragement and inspiration given by our current clergy, Michael and Liz.

Introduction

When we asked the past and present clergy of the Hempnall Group to write their reflections on their ministry, to commemorate the fiftieth anniversary of the Group, we little realised what a feast of wisdom would be released.

Taking as their starting-point the writers' time in these parishes, these essays describe where they came from to the Group, or where they went on to, or both. But this book tells a bigger story, as they have used the experience gained both here and elsewhere to reflect on changing roles within the Church of England during the last half-century.

Anthony Lathe, who laid the foundations of the Group with Peter Bradshaw and Mark Fitzwilliams, considers the changing face of professionals.

After the initial trio moved on, they were followed by Cedric Bradbury and Michael Woods, who did much to enhance the involvement of the laity.

Cedric instituted a team of lay preachers to assist with services. Two members of this team have contributed to this book: George Levack has given an overview of his experience in the Group, having now moved away, and Colin Way, who was later ordained, explores the role of the laity.

Enid Gray, whose husband Kenneth Gray did sterling work as a retired minister, has described her experience of living in one of the parishes over this period and for many years after. Sadly, she did not live to see this book published. Her daughter has kindly provided us with the biographical information that follows her article.

Stuart Nairn, who came next and is the only one of our contributors apart from the current clergy still working as a stipendiary clergyman, paints a picture of changing teams and the importance of lay involvement. Peter Moss, who helped us celebrate the twenty-fifth anniversary of the Group, focuses on the value of a team of clergy and laity and the importance of continuity. Keith James highlights the challenge of working in a team.

Ernest Green speaks of the effect of moving from the old parochial system. Conal Mahony stresses the value of providing continuity, and emphasises the theological underpinning of the concept of group ministry.

Finally, Liz Billett and Michael Kingston, the clergy serving here as we approach our fiftieth anniversary, tell us what they value in what they have inherited, and illustrate the ways in which they are building on what went before.

The Hempnall Group was founded in 1964, on the initiative of Bishop Launcelot Fleming, not just as an expedient but to enrich the lives of those living in these quiet villages. In 2003 we marked the fortieth anniversary of the Group by publishing a book, *Beyond the Parish Pump*, which gave an extensive description of how it had developed over the years. The essays collected here give an indication of how this vision has developed not only in this Group but also in a wider context.

A small note on terminology: the body known as the Group Council was officially renamed the Team Council when the legal constitution of the Group was adopted in 1991. However, both terms have continued to be current, and are interchangeable in general usage.

Jill Turner and Sarah Patey
August 2013

Are the Clergy 'Professional'?

Anthony Lathe

In fifty years so much has changed—not least in the perception of the role of Church of England clergy in Church and society. It is not just about the expectations people have of clergy, but how clergy themselves see what it is they are supposed to be doing.

When I came to the churches in what became the Hempnall Group in late 1962 there was only one style of worship, *The Book of Common Prayer*. Some of us felt a bit daring if we changed a word or two to bring it up to date. Clergy in the countryside were presumed to be elderly and certainly in our part of Norfolk they seemed to be. I went to the farewell service of one who was retiring at the age of ninety; he was as lively as a cricket. I learnt that some people in the Group called me 'the boy parson'. And of course there were only one or two parishes for each clergyman. Women were not on the scene. The ideal was for the clergyman to be in charge of his parish and, on the whole, churchwardens and church councils accepted that. Clergy paid their own working expenses and contributed with others to the maintenance of the buildings. The vicar was expected to visit his people, to know them, and to take part in and contribute to village life, in addition to his duties in church. Fifty years ago it was becoming apparent that this ideal could not continue much longer.

What to do? A number of possibilities were open. One might be to ordain lots of people, with minimal training. to work as clergy, perhaps part-time, without pay. But the clergy were a learned profession and many thought that a proper training appropriate for a profession was essential. This involved, ideally, a degree, two years' residential training in theology and ministry, or a three year residential course followed by five years of supervision in parishes as a curate, before being given the independence of responsibility for a parish. Fifty years ago this ideal was already compromised with schemes such as the non-residential Southwark Ordination Course. To ordain people who did not fulfil those exacting professional standards was thought by many to be unacceptable. Attitudes of other clergy, particularly senior clergy, to those trained on part-time courses are well described by Dr John Edmondson in his important and comprehensive study of regional theological courses and their effectiveness.[1] In our discussions with the Mission de France, for example, we learnt that the worker priests were traditionally trained priests who became workers. This was true of the few Anglican worker priests in Britain.[2] There would be practical difficulties with worker priests in charge of parishes, such as decisions about who would take the funerals during working hours, or which job would have priority if there was a conflict.

A second possibility could be to continue the old system but to add more and more parishes to each clergyman. The objection to this was that it would be impossible to maintain the ideal of the pastoral, visiting parson, apart from the necessity of cutting down the number of services in different churches so he could get round. The old system could be maintained if parishes were grouped together with some churches being closed but, as you can imagine, that was thought to be a non-starter.

A third possibility was openly to acknowledge the problem and alter the system. Parishes could be grouped together and clergy could work in teams. With mutual support the clergy could manage a greater workload and parishes could help one another. Professionally this would mirror what was happening, for example, in general medical practice at the time, in the development of group practices. It could also open the way for some clergy to work part-time in the parishes as they could be covered by their full-time colleagues.

When I was in training there was to my knowledge only one team ministry in the English countryside. It was the South Ormsby Group of twelve parishes in Lincolnshire. It was started in 1949. It is interesting that A.C. Smith's book written about it ten years later was entitled *The South Ormsby Experiment*.[3] Still an experiment after ten years! As someone who wanted to work in the countryside, full of the ideals of the seventeenth-century poet and clergyman George Herbert,[4] it seemed to me a modern and sensible way forward. But

---

[1] John James William Edmondson, *A History of the Regional Theological Courses and an Evaluation of their Effectiveness in the Initial Training of the Clergy of the Church of England* (PhD thesis, University of Durham, 2003).

[2] John Mantle, *Britain's First Worker Priests* (London: SCM Press, 2000).

[3] A.C. Smith, *The South Ormsby Experiment* (London: SPCK, 1960).

[4] George Herbert, *A Priest to the Temple, or, The Country Parson his Character and Rule of Holy Life* (1632).

there was no opportunity for a young man. I did a short curacy in Yorkshire and applied to the South Ormsby Group, who would have had me. But in 1961 the Hilborough Group was established in the Brecklands of Norfolk, and it was known that Norfolk was keen to develop group ministry. So I wrote to the Bishop of Norwich, and the rest is history. In 1963 groups were planned and formed at Hempnall, Sandringham and Raveningham. Trunch and Barnham Broom soon followed, with Brinton and Blakeney. After 1965 eight more groups were set up. The group ministry pattern, therefore, spread widely through the Norfolk countryside. Arthur Smith's hope that his experiment would encourage others was not in vain, and there was plenty of opportunity for younger clergy to work in the countryside.

If the truth be known, we in group ministry thought this was it. We studied scripture and found team ministry there. We went to conferences. We constantly met each other. We formed a good relationship with the Mission de France, who had teams of worker priests in grouped parishes in the French countryside. In our style of group ministry (technically, *team* ministry) we said the daily offices together, we planned together, we shared the many tasks of the parish clergy between us and we took part in and contributed to village life, getting to know as many individuals and families as possible. It meant long hours and hard work. It was certainly very costly to family and personal life.

At the same time the finances of the church needed attending to. It was no longer possible to coast along hoping for a gift or legacy, depending on the minimal contributions from the parishioners, or even the occasional farmer dipping into his back pocket and saying, 'Do something good with this!'[5] The clergy were being paid better than they had been before but it was apparent that, even so, they could no longer afford all the expenses of their work even if it was right to ask them to meet those costs. Certainly the grouping of parishes helped towards a solution of the financial problem. This was because richer parishes began to help poorer ones with their obligations, and a central group fund was set up to meet clergy and

[5] In the Hempnall Group the average giving of people on the church electoral roll was a penny farthing; regular communicants contributed an average of 1s 8d (12p in decimal currency): Anthony Russell (ed.), *Groups and Teams in the Countryside* (London: SPCK, 1975), p. 62.

other general group expenses. In worship itself new forms of service were being introduced. We felt easy in using forms which were more interesting and imaginative and seasonally appropriate. Also the churches coming together from time to time could create a grand occasion which the weekly Sunday service in an individual parish could not hope to do.

The first ten years were perhaps halcyon days. Ten years of graft and change which enabled the plant not only to survive but to develop and grow further. As a building reflects the pattern of its foundation, so it is not surprising that on my occasional visits back, the Hempnall Group seems to me to have the same atmosphere as it did, say, forty-five years ago, although both the villages and the churches have changed a lot.

That was then. The pressure was still on and times still changing when I was asked to form the Quidenham Group in 1972. This began with some keen parishes, some reluctant parishes, and part of a group which had broken up. The ideals of the country clergyman were still there in the background, but for me it meant beginning again. It was hard to understand again the disappointment felt, the reluctance to give up some of the independence of the individual parishes for the sake of an uncertain future. But perhaps in a gentler and less interesting way we did it. Then I was not Peter Bradshaw, the Hempnall Group rector, and my colleagues were more experienced in ministry than Mark Fitzwilliams or I, as team vicars, had been. Essentially our aims were the same: to provide a balanced and varied professional ministry across the group of parishes; to co-operate to solve problems, such as finance, which could not be solved locally; to provide an imaginative variety of appropriate worship with the opportunities for big occasions; to be engaged with the local community, individuals and groups.

It had been clear for years that the number of full-time paid clergy would decrease and so we tried to prepare for that. When the time came at last, after I had left the Quidenham Group, it was gratifying that two local people were ordained for ministry in the group. At his ordination one of them said to me, 'You know, Anthony, it is twenty years ago you first suggested that I should be ordained'. As in the Hempnall Group, we endeavoured to encourage lay participation and decision-making at both group and local level.

After ten more years or so it was time to move on. I did not want to do it all over again. My wife yearned for the town—pavements and street lights—so we went to the inner suburbs of Norwich. One church, one vicar, one congregation, but no real sense of a wider community. Compared with the countryside where the vicar was part of the scene I was no longer a figure of interest, and although the church building was large, few people I met actually knew it, although almost all could name the pub next door.[6] It was a different kind of ministry. As always, though, the church produces stars, really good committed people who provide the bedrock of parish and congregational life. I was also fortunate to work with two brilliant, part-time women curates. After a further ten years or so we moved to Sheringham on the North Norfolk coast. This is a seaside resort with a strong local community so, in a kind of way, it combined the community aspects of ministry in the countryside with the more congregational focus of the city. It was a good and encouraging finale.

Gradually over the years the style of ministry changed. Not only were women ordained; the expectation became that ministry was more collaborative, not just with other clergy, in teams, but with lay people also becoming more involved and responsible. It was increasingly recognised that clergy should have some time for their families and themselves. It also became more informal and more fun; both features we tried to encourage in the early days of the Hempnall Group. I remember talking to some youngsters about why young people did not come to church, and one of them said 'terror of vicars'. Later, I recall the first time a child of about three called me by my Christian name in church.

Out of this latter remembrance comes a kind of ambivalence which has to do with the concept of profession. Questions arise such as, is the concept an appropriate one at all for describing clergy? How professional are the clergy? Are there—or should there be—different kinds of clergy with different degrees of professionalism? To put it bluntly, is being a parish priest a job of work or a way of life? Certainly my feeling is that over the past fifty years it has taken on more and more of the characteristics of a job.

I need to elaborate on this. There is a huge literature on occupations and professions, and not a little about clergy. But

[6] The church is still there and active; the pub has closed and is now a Chinese restaurant!

broadly we can say that a professional has specialised knowledge and skills. This has to do with the depth and breadth of training. A professional is chosen by others in the same line to join the profession. This has to do with initial selection, continuous monitoring and examination during training, and a final recognition of joining. After joining, the professional is expected to behave in certain recognised ways, to conduct relationships with those he or she deals with according to professional ethics. This is particularly true of the 'caring' professions, as the professional often deals with people on a one-to-one basis. So it is a job, but it involves a way of life. The caring professional has to be the kind of person who can relate appropriately to the people being dealt with. Misbehaviour, not necessarily technical incompetence, can lead to dismissal and being forbidden to practise. There is recognition of the profession by society, which will forbid those attempting to pass themselves off, when they are not, as members of a particular profession.

If we take medicine as an example, a medical doctor follows a full academic study of medicine, including practical work—years working in a junior capacity under supervision in hospital treating patients. That is before, for example, specialising in hospital medicine or going into general practice. This pattern was set in the nineteenth century. From the middle of that century, with the establishment of residential theological colleges,[7] clergy went through more or less the same kind of process.

This pattern of training was roughly the one I went through in the early 1960s. I studied for three years at university, and two years of four terms each year at a residential theological college. Here the training was mostly academic theology. People who had not attended university did three years at a theological college. There was little practical training in how to do the job, but a lot of personal training. Because they were small, rather closed communities, one was being brought up, formed even, into being a member of the clergy. The principal of a theological college was a father-figure. The practical training was expected to come later, in two curacies involving professional supervision and training by a senior clergyman in a parish. The minimum for each separate curacy would normally be two years. So it would typically take nine years before a person was

[7] See Anthony Russell, *The Clerical Profession* (London: SPCK, 1980).

given responsibility as an independent parish priest after being accepted for training. If the goal of the 'professional' priest was to have a parish of his own, team rectors and vicars gave that ideal up. In this they were doing no more than they were asking parishes to do, to give up something of their own independence. I note from a recent prospectus of one part-time course that one of the 'programme objectives' of the curriculum offered is 'to be able to work collaboratively and to facilitate the ministry of others'.[8] Is there a better description of what we set out to do fifty years ago?

With the kind of training people of my generation had had and, no doubt, the social background of many clergy, which was characteristically 'professional', it was not surprising to be treated as a professional person. Hence the 'terror of vicars' and not expecting to be called by your Christian name by a young child! You will already have picked up something of how this professional image was being eroded, not least by the clergy themselves. As more and more decisions were handed to lay people, so the authority of the clergy was diminished. As the clergy became more dependent on the laity to get things done; as lay people became more involved in the selection of clergy to parishes; as the clergy became more informal, so the professional image was being gradually replaced by one that was more and more dependent on the personality of the individual. It was no surprise then that a three-year-old recognised me as a person, addressing me by name in church. As a matter of fact, among those who had been studying the role of the clergy in an academic way there had been some who doubted that the word 'profession' should be applied to the clergy at all.[9] This was because the way in which clergy performed was seen to be dependent less on particular, specialised trained skills and knowledge than on their personal qualities.

However, what we may now call the 'de-professionalisation' of clergy had been encouraged by a number of other factors. The old method of training was very expensive. Expenditure would be reduced if people could be trained on part-time courses while living at home, or could be doing a state-subsidised university degree with

---

[8] St Mellitus College, *Student Handbook 2010-2011*, p. 46.

[9] See, for example, Robert Towler and APM Coxon, *The Fate of the Anglican Clergy* (London: Macmillan, 1979).

an attachment to a college which supervised potential clergy. Also, more recently, there has been a huge growth in knowledge available through the internet. The specialised knowledge on which different professions depended was becoming available to everyone.[10] In the Church younger people were either not coming forward for ordination or were actively discouraged from doing so until they had some 'life experience'. As older people came forward and were accepted for training they could continue in work, supporting their families while training at weekends and in the evenings. The spin-off from this has been a boom in part-time training. Now well over half the clergy are trained in this way. Further, the training years are shortened into three terms, with a week's summer course. Three months are also lost because ordination tends to come earlier in the final year, in June rather than September. There has obviously been a considerable shortening of the time the individual spends learning specialised knowledge before practising. In other words, people training for the clergy are learning less theology than they used to.[11] The intense, supervised formation of clergy in a residential situation is considerably diminished. Because older people, and often married people, are being ordained, they need to achieve the responsibility, and pay, of parish priests earlier than used to be the case, so curacy, initial professional supervision, has been shortened, with many doing just one curacy of three years. Other features of a profession are still in place, such as recognition by the state and admission being controlled by members of the profession. Individual professional independence is still a feature, although talking to clergy you get the feeling that it is gradually being eroded by the organisation, making them feel more and more like employees.

This is just to give a flavour of what has been going on in the clerical profession over the past fifty years. It is different, but it is not all bad. For a start, realistically, the church could not support the old system; it was too expensive. Then, many mature people would not be received into the clergy; indeed, perhaps there would be very few people going in at all. If it is true that the clergy depend, as they always depended, more on their personal qualities than on their

---

[10] A doctor, for example, may be dealing with a patient who has thoroughly researched their own particular problem and its treatment before arriving in the surgery.

[11] Edmondson, *Regional Theological Courses*, goes into considerable detail on this.

knowledge and trained skills, then to recruit mature people seems eminently sensible. As there is plenty of theological information available on the internet, clergy can use this in their preaching and teaching, making it personal and appropriate to their particular situation. They no longer need that long training in theological knowledge. As the feeling that the 'professional' is in charge and knows best recedes, so the church itself becomes much more cooperative and egalitarian.

There are, though, some aspects of profession which may, importantly, remain to inform the individual's work and status, although it may be that these too are being eroded. I will briefly look at access, confidentiality, and personality.

In the concept of profession there is the idea that the professional is open to everyone. A doctor will see anyone who wishes to have a consultation, and a member of the clergy will see anyone who wants to come. If fixed surgery times and out-of-hours medical services have protected doctors from their patients' demands, clergy have been less able to erect barriers. Their personal telephone number is usually readily available to everyone; where they live is easily identifiable. My feeling is that this is still how many clergy see themselves, at the beck and call of everyone. An erosion of availability is now taking place because of pressure of time, as clergy become fewer on the ground, are increasingly involved in administration, and have greater focus on the congregation rather than the whole parish. Certainly, when I began, we went out of our way to increase the sense of availability. I spent at least every afternoon and several evenings a week visiting people either at their own or at other people's request, and sometimes simply going round getting to know the people of the parishes, regardless of their church affiliation. This was expected. It was extremely rare not to be invited into someone's home when you called. It is also now recognised that clergy need time off for further training, for retreats and for recreation—further examples of how clergy are becoming less available and open to everyone.

In the concept of 'profession' there is also the idea that what is said to the professional is confidential, person to person—the doctor and his patient, the lawyer and her client. This is compromised in many professions by note-taking and the sharing of those notes with others; the availability of those notes to administrative staff and others; consulting on case histories; and even mentoring as, for example, counsellors are mentored. It may be that the clergy are the only ones left who keep this kind of confidentiality, and I do not mean just within the confines of the sacrament of confession. Certainly I have felt it improper to discuss individuals with other clergy or, indeed, with anyone else. If I made notes it was done with permission and openly. The erosion of confidentiality may be taking place because of more cooperation between clergy (this was one of the fears of team ministry), or the idea that the vicar and partner are one unit and that they should share everything. Someone who marries a member of the clergy may expect there always to be a hidden part of their partner's life. It must be a problem for couples when one of them becomes a member of the clergy after doing another job when what has happened at work was a feature of marital conversation.

One aspect of the idea of profession is that it is a way of life centred around a task. In the 'caring' professions, certainly, the character of a professional is felt to be very important. The selection process for clergy is designed to weed out those who might prove unacceptable not just from lack of ability or commitment, but for not having the right kind of character. Personal examination and reflection are important elements in training and are heavily emphasised in the prospectuses and practices of the part-time courses.

In this chapter, from my experience, I have hinted at some of the changes that have been taking place over the past fifty years. If the idea of the clergy being 'professionals' seems a less accurate description of them than it used to be, it remains a helpful peg on which to hang a discussion of the role of the clergy in society. To be a member of the clergy is still a demanding, challenging, interesting, worthwhile, and sometimes fun occupation. For me it is a privilege to have been part of so many people's lives in all kinds of circumstances.

After a brief curacy in Yorkshire Anthony Lathe spent all his ministry in Norfolk. After the Hempnall Group he went to set up the Quidenham Group. He then went to the inner suburbs of Norwich for eleven years and finished his full-time career in the seaside town of Sheringham. He and his wife Carla have a married daughter and three grandchildren and all live in Hertfordshire. Apart from interests around his work, he has researched the development of professionals working together in groups. He was a keen cyclist, making a number of long trips in Europe. He now gardens, helps locally in the church and works with children in the primary school who are beginning to read.

Eight and a Half Glorious Years

Stuart Nairn

It was in March 1980 that Susan and I came to live in the Hempnall Group at The Vicarage, Triple Plea Road, Woodton. We were about to celebrate our first wedding anniversary. I had just finished a three and a half year stint as curate of East Dereham in Norfolk. Susan had been brought up at East Dereham and the move from familiar surroundings was a huge experience for her.

We made the decision to come to the Hempnall Group having turned down the offer that I should become the incumbent of Fiskerton to the east of Lincoln City—a living in the gift of the Dean and Chapter of Peterborough Cathedral. The major reason for our decision was the opportunity/the gift that we saw in working alongside Canon Cedric Bradbury—the then Rector of the Hempnall Group. His enthusiasm, his commitment and his joy were infectious and we never regretted the decision for me to come and serve as team vicar. The practice of second curacies was dying out and Cedric was committed to the principle that priests were equal, whether rector or team vicar. A principle that senior staff in the diocese struggled to accept, insisting in those days that a team vicar should have been in orders for seven years.

Our first day was but an illustration of the hospitality we were to receive in our eight and a half years of ministry in the Hempnall Group. The day of our move from East Dereham the gas board had decided to dig a ditch across our exit so we were running late by the time we arrived in Woodton. Our first visitor was the local head teacher—Joe Kerruish—a Manx man who came bearing a parcel of food from the parishioners to welcome us into our new home. Joe was married to Margaret and they became lifelong friends, sadly both departed now. Soon after his visit came the neighbours from next door but one, Ken and Enid Gray. Ken was a retired priest of many years' experience, and he and his wife became good friends and important guides in our ministry in the Group. On the other side were Bob and Kath Boyce. I later discovered that Bob was a very distant relative on my mother's side. Bob was a tremendous guide in sharing his knowledge and his produce from his vegetable garden.

We came very quickly to learn we were among friends and for that reason our years in Woodton were glorious years.

There were great characters in the Group at the time—organists such as Connie Tye (Hempnall), Eva Mainstone (Woodton and Bedingham), Mabel Whitham (Fritton), Dorothy Wheelhouse (Morningthorpe) and Margaret Alden (Hardwick and Shelton). Farmers such as Jack and Joan Easton at Manor Farm, Woodton, the Harrold family of Bedingham and Topcroft, Theo and Ivy Gooch at Bedingham, Harry and Janet Holden of Home Farm, Woodton, and their son Richard and Jeanie Holden of Priory Farm, Bedingham, the Alexanders of Hardwick and Shelton, the Sargents of Morningthorpe, and Robert and Jane Crawford at Topcroft. I later discovered that Robert was a distant relative, from Scotland, on my father's side. The saying seems true that you are only seven handshakes away from someone you know and that Norfolk is a small village. Even here in the Nar Valley Group where we live now Susan is a distant cousin to the local undertaker and her great grandfather is buried in Pentney churchyard!

It was in the Hempnall Group that our two children, Fiona and Andrew were born and baptised into the Christian Church—Fiona at Woodton and Andrew at Bedingham. Susan and I offer much thanks for the kindness of many parishioners and neighbours who held us in their embrace as we learnt the skills of early parenthood and also travelled the pain of the loss of a third child in miscarriage. Now those two children are grown up—Fiona working for the UEA and passionate about the life and history of the people of Australia. Andrew working back stage in the theatre at the Nottingham Playhouse as stage technician—he is now married, living in Derby, and in turn learning the skills of parenthood with our first grandchild Clara.

When we came for the interview before joining the Hempnall Group Cedric showed us around the Group—each church with its own story and history. Topcroft stands out from that day—the verger/cleaner was Dolly Fisher (sister of Lennie Andrews, our milkman in Woodton and a member of Woodton Methodist Church). Dolly kept the key but to get to it we had to run the gauntlet of the geese. When we arrived at the church porch we were greeted with a week's worth of rooks' twigs. Cedric's view was that it was quite likely that this church would not survive the following years. How wrong we have both been proved! This church has flourished over the years and there has developed a tremendous sense of community in the village.

For those such as ourselves coming into an established and lively group of parishes, it was difficult for us to truly understand what it was like prior to the formation of the Group—with no resident clergy left, small congregations, and mouldy kneelers and hymn books. There is an apocryphal story that Peter Bradshaw picked up a mouldy hymnbook, saying 'Is this worthy of God? NO!' and throwing it across the church. Change was afoot and we came as inheritors of a great tradition that had been established. Even today it is difficult for people new to the Group to understand why it is important to hold onto the value of working as a group rather than simply being eight independent villages and churches. This is as true of the Nar Valley Group where I am now based as it is of the Hempnall Group as it approaches its fiftieth anniversary. So much more can be achieved by working together—opportunities such as working parties to decorate the churches, summer holiday camps to entertain and share the faith with the young, or Shelton Christmas Concerts bringing glorious music into the countryside. Indeed many of the principles that I learnt in the Hempnall Group have shaped the foundations of the Nar Valley Group, now in its fifteenth year.

As with any journey, there are those tough moments. The first of those came at the end of our first year when Cedric announced that the Bishop had asked him to go and be the Vicar of Wroxham and that he had accepted the invitation. He expressed his confidence in my ability to carry the Group forward but I knew that there was a huge weight of tradition and good practice that rested upon my shoulders. The following eighteen months were demanding, as I endeavoured to maintain the worship in all eight churches with the help of the ministry team that had been established, and responding to the requests for the occasional offices of baptisms, marriages and funerals. While I was away on holiday the Bishop announced the appointment of the next rector—Jeffery Smith, who was moving from within the diocese and whose experience included working in South Africa in Kimberley and Kuruman diocese, as well as in the Episcopal Church of Scotland. The pattern of working within the Hempnall Group was a new challenge for Jeffery, which he took some time to adjust to, as in those years this was still regarded as a pioneering pattern of organising the Church of England in the countryside.

When Jeffery left after just a few years, we were once again thrown into a vacancy and once again I went away on holiday only to find the Diocese seeking to fill the vacancy in my absence. This time the proposed rector was a former colleague from my East Dereham days, Peter Moss. Peter insisted that he would not accept the position until we had opportunity to speak together. He was aware of the importance of colleagues being able to work together. We spoke and Peter arrived and another chapter opened in the life of the Group. During Peter's time we celebrated the twenty-first anniversary of the Group; we saw Colin Way ordained priest for the non-stipendiary ministry and welcomed Keith James as a curate to be trained in rural ministry.

In the wider church the Sea of Faith movement was becoming established as a result of the writings and questionings of Don Cupitt—*The Myth of God Incarnate* and similar writings shook the foundations of theological understanding. The Church found it hard to allow priests such as Peter, with his enquiring mind, to remain in the Church. For me that would mean a third vacancy, and there was still no prospect of the senior staff thinking that a team vicar could become rector within the parishes where he was serving.

Such short-sightedness seems archaic now that the church places curates after three years of ordained ministry into incumbencies on their own. The hierarchy decided that I should move on to a new position. Even then this was not an easy task, and indeed it has become increasingly difficult over the years for clergy to move, as we have shifted from the Bishop pointing you in a particular direction to the now more familiar process of responding to advertisements and entering a competitive interview process. One wonders how much opportunity is given to listen to the guiding of the Holy Spirit. I am far from convinced that this new process produces any better appointments.

It is now some twenty-four years since we left the Hempnall Group to come to West Norfolk. The landscape of the Church of England has changed considerably and is constantly evolving. In some respects it is a very different ministry that young ordinands enter into. The backdrop of society has become much more secular in outlook and old norms and customs have given way to data protection, health and safety and accountability—including ministerial reviews which are focused on competence to do the job.

Ministry in schools is also changing and government policies at the present time place a real question mark against the continuance of church schools and the ability for parish priests to enter into the school environment. We see small rural schools entering into partnerships and federations under one head teacher and one governing body, as the 'magic number' for survival is now put at 210 pupils.

Small rural churches are also under pressure from financial targets. There is a generation of worshippers now aged over seventy-five, and many wonder where the next generation will come from. New initiatives in mission and worship are offered under the title of Fresh Expressions and Messy Church, but whether these will last the span of time is yet to be tested. New styles of ordained ministry have emerged with Non-Stipendiary and Ordained Local Ministry clergy, and now both men and women can be priests.

As I write this in mid-2012, we await the announcement this autumn of a new Archbishop of Canterbury to guide the Anglican Communion and to lead the Church of England. The dear old C of E is heading for choppy waters over the question of the Ordination of Women as Bishops and Same Sex Marriages in church; there seems little doubt that the shape of the Church of England will change in the coming years and probably quite radically.

Yet that was what was said fifty years ago when the Hempnall Group and other groups and teams came into being. Many saw it as the beginning of the end and yet in this book we prepare to celebrate fifty years of continuing ministry in the villages of the Hempnall Group. Years which have seen vibrancy, new life breathed into our village churches and communities, and a sharing of ministry with the laity, releasing their vocation for Christian discipleship. Yes, we ask, what will the next fifty years be like? But trusting in God we go forward with that same resolve as those early founders of the Group that our vocation is to proclaim the gospel, to minister to those whom God has given us and to offer worship before God as he feeds us with his Son Jesus Christ in bread and wine.

As I draw into the last decade of my active paid ministry I look back and rejoice at the foundations that were laid by my title vicar, Jeremy Saville, in East Dereham and my year with Cedric Bradbury in the Hempnall Group. They were tough teachers but they taught me a great deal and so did many parishioners and friends in the Hempnall Group, things which I have been able to draw upon in these subsequent years; lessons which have stood me in good stead as we have brought the Nar Valley Group into being and breathed new life into seven more rural churches, this time in West Norfolk.

Church conventions mean that when a priest moves on he or she makes room for those who come after them. It does not mean that those bonds of friendship are forgotten. Rather, they are held in prayer before God as we recall times of laughter and of tears, of joy and sorrow in ministry and in life and death. May the coming years see the Hempnall Group continue to flourish and to enrich the life of the wider church with its important message of working together for the greater good of the kingdom.

God bless you all—those who remember us and those who have come afterwards.

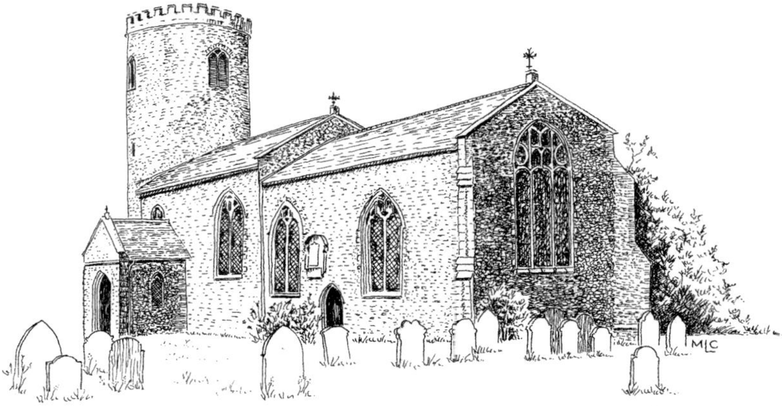

Morningthorpe church

Stuart Nairn

Stuart Nairn left HMSO in Norwich to study theology at King's College London and Canterbury, and was ordained to serve in the Dereham Association of Parishes in Norfolk. He became team vicar to the Hempnall Group in 1980. Stuart and Susan's children, Fiona and Andrew, were born at Woodton. Stuart moved in 1988 to Narborough and Pentney near to Swaffham, serving as rural dean of Lynn between 1991 and 1999. In 1997 he became additionally responsible for Castle Acre and surrounding parishes. In 2011 the Nar Valley Group of Parishes was formally established. In 2003 Stuart became an honorary canon of Norwich Cathedral, and in 2006 rural dean of Breckland. He holds a Master of Theology from University of Wales—Lampeter. He is a Fellow of the Royal Society of Arts.

All Are Called

Colin Way

In 1985 the Church of England published a series of essays under the title of *All are Called*. It was a working party's attempt to set out the church's thinking on a theology of the laity in the light of the way in which lay people were developing their responsibilities as Christians in everyday life, both at home and at work, and their participation in the life of their local churches. Members of the working party wanted to affirm the New Testament teaching about vocation that had been rediscovered in the previous thirty years—that all are called by God to be servants and ministers and citizens of the Kingdom. All are called to be the body of Christ on earth now—bishops, priests and laity together.

This calling—this shared vocation—has been characteristic of the worship, ministry and mission within the Hempnall Group, and it seems right therefore to celebrate and describe its development in this series of fiftieth anniversary essays.

We are all called, all our days, to strive for a special quality of living, a kind of 'saintliness', a thoughtful, compassionate goodness. We all have gifts to be developed and used in God's service. This is at the heart of the Gospel and also at the heart of the New Testament model of ministry. For the early Christians, the church was a community, a fellowship—it was *all* the people of God. We can find St Paul's teaching on this in Romans 12, Ephesians 4 and 1 Corinthians 12. J.B. Phillips, in a fine colloquial translation of Paul's words, reminds us of this teaching in his *Letters to Young Christians*:

> For just as you have many members in one physical body and those members differ in their functions, so we, though many in number, comprise one Body in Christ and are all members of one another. Through the grace of God we have different gifts. If our gift is preaching, let us preach to the limit of our vision. If it is serving others let us concentrate on our service. If it is teaching let us give all we have to our teaching; and if our gift be the stimulating of the faith of others let us set ourselves to it. Let the man who is called to give, give freely; let the man who wields authority think of his responsibility; and let the sick visitor do his job cheerfully.

Colin Way

My wife and I, together with our three young daughters, came to live in the village of Topcroft in 1975. I had already heard of the visionary nature of the Hempnall Group—inspired and led by Peter Bradshaw—and was glad that we had found a house in one of the eight villages that made up the Group. Although Peter Bradshaw had moved to be a residentiary canon at Norwich Cathedral by the time I arrived as a parishioner, it soon became clear to me that his New Testament vision of ministry—building up a spirit of community fellowship (*koinonia*) and the sharing of talents, time and money (stewardship)—had already helped to establish a sense of common bonding in what had previously been eight separate and disparate parishes. They were now beginning to work together as never before—learning to share in worship and ministry. Parishioners from all the villages were also taking their share of parish and group tasks—not leaving it all for the clergy to do. They were helping to run holiday clubs, summer working parties, magazine production and distribution, collections for Christian Aid, Lent house groups, church music, and many other and various administrative tasks.

Peter Bradshaw's vision of ministry—the building up the 'whole body of Christ'—was to be continued under the wise and thoughtful leadership of Cedric Bradbury, who succeeded him as team rector.

Cedric expressed the view quite early in his leadership that the next step forward for the Hempnall Group should be the development of lay ministry. He was very concerned that the original team of three full-time stipendiary priests had already been reduced to two, and that there was a possibility that when the team vicar, Michael Woods, moved on there might not be a full-time replacement for him. Then, as now, there was a shortage of clergy, especially of clergy wanting to work in rural areas, and a severe shortage of money to pay for them. But Cedric was not only influenced by the practical need to enlarge the ministry team, he also believed very strongly that his priestly ministry should be shared with laymen and women. He supported the views expressed in Hans-Ruedi Weber's booklet *Salty Christians*:

> Too often the clergy undertake to fulfil by themselves the ministry of the Church. And too often the laity delegate their ministry to one man—the clergyman. This 'one man show' is deeply unbiblical. Christ does not grant special gifts only to men and women who are full-time, lifetime employees of the Church. All the people of God share in

> Christ's ministry in and to the world. Of course, the clergyman is chosen by God for certain important functions in the Church, and for these functions he is 'ordained'. One of these important functions is to nourish, equip, help and sustain the laity for their ministry.

These were the circumstances that encouraged Cedric Bradbury to set up a small study group, of which I was to be a member, to consider how we might best develop lay ministry. So in a report to the Group Council it was recommended, and later agreed, that Cedric should set about the task 'calling out' those who had the respect, support and understanding of their local Christian communities to be members of a new pastoral ministry team—a partnership of lay and ordained. It was also recommended that those called out for this form of lay ministry should be appropriately trained and prepared, just as the clergy were prepared and trained for their task of ministry. It was also agreed that just as the clergy received a form of official recognition and commissioning at their ordination, so too should our lay ministers be officially recognised and commissioned by the Bishop at the end of their training.

So it was that during 1979 nine lay men and women were called to serve as lay ministers, and a rigorous two-year programme of training was devised and put into practice. This programme covered Old and New Testament studies, public and private prayer, aspects of liturgy, visiting and other associated pastoral matters. In many ways the course was not so different from the one that Lay Readers followed and Ordained Local Ministers follow today—but we believed at the time that what we wanted was our own locally based programme which would build up our own ministry team.

Happily, when Michael Woods left the Group in 1979 the Bishop was able to find the money to appoint a replacement. Stuart Nairn was recruited from Dereham and instituted as team vicar in 1980, just in time to help with the completion of our training programme and to be there when Bishop Maurice Wood finally commissioned the ministry team at Shelton church in 1982.

Subsequently, the newly commissioned ministry team met regularly with the rector and team vicar once a month for prayer and discussion of theological and pastoral concerns. Later, we set out a more formal description of the role of members of the ministry team:

> The lay ministry team of the Hempnall Group shares with the ordained ministry in the witness, ministry and mission of the church:

> Members of the Ministry Team share in the ministry of prayer. They are to be faithful in Sunday worship and private prayer, and endeavour to join in other acts of weekly group worship and quiet days as they are able.
>
> They are to share in the min stry of leading worship. They will take it in turns to lead the Ministry of the Word and Intercessions at Group services, and are authorised to administer the chalice at Holy Communion. They may be asked to do the same at parish services, and, if a priest is not present, to read the Morning or Evening Prayer, and to lead Family Services.
>
> The Ministry Team will meet regularly to read and study the Bible and other Christian books. They should be prepared to take part in Group weekends and discussion groups, and other educational enterprises, especially among the young.
>
> Members of the Ministry Team may also play their part in the ministry of administration in their parishes and in the Group. Some members of the team are elected as parochial representatives to the Group Council and its committees, but all members are ex-officio members of the Council and may serve on one of the committees of their choice.
>
> Members of the team are authorised to share with the clergy in the ministry of visiting. These visits will cover both specific matters, such as welcoming newcomers, baptism, anniversaries, sickness, special need or bereavement, and the more generalised task of regular visitation of every home on the church's list. These visits are reported at meetings of the Ministry Team.
>
> Members of the team will play their part in the ministry of reconciliation, helping to bring people together, and fostering fellowship and good will in their parishes. They are to be the ears and eyes of the ordained clergy and seek their help in all matters spiritual.
>
> All members of the team will give a very high priority to the monthly meetings of the team and be subject to a review every three years by local PCCs, by the Group Council and by the Bishop.

It was my good fortune to be a part of this development during the late 1970s and 1980s. Looking back, I think this form of shared ministry well suited the Hempnall Group. There was a genuine sharing and working together between lay and ordained, and a general acceptance of lay ministry in the parishes. We did, I think, play our small part in the movement that was reflected in the report that was quoted at the beginning of this article—*All are Called: Towards a Theology of the Laity*. And I think that perhaps we also played a small part in encouraging other parishes to develop their own ministry teams as this kind of collaborative ministry is now widely practised in our diocese.

Colin Way was educated at Wallington County Grammar School and St Catharine's College Cambridge. Between school and university he served two years in the Royal Navy. The first 30 years of his working life were spent in education—first as a teacher, then as headmaster of a grammar school and finally as Chief Inspector of Schools in Norfolk. Colin was active in the Hempnall Group from 1975 to 1987. He was churchwarden of Topcroft parish church and chairman of the Group Council from 1979 to 1984. In 1984 he was ordained at Norwich Cathedral as a non-stipendiary minister, helping to forward the work of God in the education service as well as in the parishes of the Group. He has spent the last thirty years in parish ministry—full-time, part-time and now as an active retired priest in Norwich. He is married to Audrey and has three married daughters and nine grandchildren.

One Plus One Makes More Than Two

Peter Moss

When I heard on the grapevine in 1984 that Jeffery Smith, the then rector, was leaving the Hempnall Group, I had a definite feeling that I might be invited to succeed him (though I was not particularly *persona grata* with Bishop Maurice Wood). And so it was. Two of the six patrons of the Group—Hugh Sargent, churchwarden and landowner of Morningthorpe and Sir Charles Mott-Radclyffe, Norfolk grandee and patron of Hempnall—invited me to lunch at the Norfolk Club. They seemed to want to produce a name before the Bishop said anything (let alone the Lord Chancellor or King's College, the other patrons). And I was appointed, first with my wife having run the gauntlet of a lively meeting of sixteen churchwardens and others under the chairmanship of Colin Way at Stuart Nairn's vicarage—teamwork in action.

The history of my ministry is an ever-closer commitment to the value of teamwork. I began in 1961 in County Durham with two two-year assistant curacies with senior priests in single one-church parishes. Vicars and curates are one sort of team.

Then in 1965 I was appointed to be the first priest-in-charge of a large new housing estate on the remote edge of Sunderland. We had the original big Victorian farmhouse to live in, and for three or four years we held the church services and other meetings and classes in our own house.

After the Second World War Sunderland surrounded itself with a round dozen of largely council-house estates, and in 1965 these estates were served by six Anglican parishes (some embryonic—known as conventional districts, still in theory attached to an older mother church—and some fully fledged). Well before I arrived the clergy of these parishes, legally quite independent of each other, had begun a pattern of mutual support. The chief manifestation of this was that eleven or twelve of us (curates were two a penny in those days) met every Tuesday for worship and breakfast (and periodically for lively evening parties) and they all regarded these as prime commitments.

Breakfast once a week does not sound much, but it led to a deep mutual friendship and trust. We were able to help each other out in all sorts of ways, especially at holiday times. We felt at home in all of the churches, especially since we were all what were then known as 'Prayer Book Catholics'. Happily the cooperation continued even when some of the incumbents moved on (one died in the odour of real sanctity), showing that a real need for love and support was being met.

You might object that I am speaking just of a clergy club. But I believe that this club, this mutual knowledge and support, made all twelve of us much happier, much better men, and thus much better able to serve our lively churches and teeming estates. We were constantly learning from each other. This 'team' had absolutely no institutional basis, but to my mind it contributed greatly to the church in Sunderland.

When we had been in Sunderland seven years, we had three children and wanted to bring them up in the country. So I began to seek a change, and I am now surprised to realise that I did not at that point restrict my search to churches with teams of clergy. To cut a long story short, we landed up in Mattishall (near Dereham in the very centre of Norfolk). Mattishall, Mattishall Burgh and Welborne were part of the Dereham Association of Parishes.

Bishop Launcelot Fleming was determined to grasp the nettle of the host of tiny Norfolk parishes staffed by isolated priests, and he was willing to push the various laws governing parishes and benefices to the limit to find a better pattern of working. When parishes became vacant, the law gave him power to suspend the benefice and to delay appointing a new vicar while he, the Bishop, planned a reorganisation.

He was a Bishop with wide contacts and he recruited charismatic and highly efficient senior priests to undertake his Norfolk experiments. Peter Bradshaw came from Harpenden to start the Hempnall Group (having first turned down a similar task at Barnham Broom) and there were other notable groups formed round Raveningham, Hilborough and Sandringham, each with a team of clergy.

Charles Plummer was tempted from the vast multi-church parish of new town Hemel Hempstead to start what was called the Dereham Association of Parishes. East Dereham is a large and important town with an imposing and historic church (and at that time two daughter churches in the suburbs). Mattishall is a substantial village about four miles away. In 1972 it had just experienced the construction of three large bungalow estates, doubling its population. Yaxham and Hockering were smaller communities, but each with much new building. North Tuddenham, Welborne and Hoe were and remain scattered country villages.

Ecclesiastically the Dereham Association was rather eccentric. Charles Plummer was Vicar of Dereham and priest-in-charge of all the other parishes. But as well as a curate living in Dereham, there were three team vicars resident in the three bigger villages, and Charles gave us almost complete independence, except that he came to preside at each church's annual meeting *and* that on Sundays all five of us ranged over the whole area. So I was responsible for Mattishall (a middle-of-the-road Anglican parish), Mattishall Burgh (a tiny evangelical afternoon congregation) and Welborne (which had been a temple of high Anglo-Catholicism, now somewhat diluted).

There was morning worship at 7.30 at Dereham church on every weekday, and each of us was expected to be there four or five times a week. On Mondays we all had breakfast and a staff meeting at Dereham Vicarage.

So far as the congregations were concerned, their awareness of being in an Association came from the fact they frequently found their services being led by one of the 'other' clergy, from the four big Association services we had every year, and from the excellent joint magazine that we produced. I had mutual knowledge, support and help from four colleagues (one of them Stuart Nairn, when he was ordained as the Dereham curate). We were able to have adequate time for holidays, retreats and study. The people heard a variety of voices, and we clergy could get to appreciate a wide cross-section of town and country people.

Once again the system survived the retirement of Charles Plummer and the comings of his two successors, though it proved difficult to integrate Honingham and East Tuddenham into the Association as clergy numbers fell. And when a determinedly independent and charismatic evangelical priest followed me into Mattishall, the days of the Association were numbered. In essence the Dereham Association (which I dearly loved) was a fairly close team serving a collection of independent parishes with just a few shared facilities and occasional shared worship. It seemed good for me and good for the parishes.

And that is what I found when I arrived at the Hempnall Group, except that here there has been much more combined worship and a much greater sharing of facilities (I think of wonderful children's weeks, the Group Council and its influential committees, and the ministry team as it was in the 1980s).

So having started my main ministry with the loose but intense fellowship of the estates clergy of Sunderland, I moved to a properly constituted but eccentric team at the Dereham Association, but still in great part presiding over a particular patch. When I came to the Hempnall Group, I found that the work of the clergy was more integrated, and though we had acknowledged 'spheres of influence', Stuart Nairn and I both went to every parish meeting, as did Keith James.

Why has the Hempnall Group prospered while others have faltered or disbanded? First, it had a Big Bang of a beginning with the great trio of Peter Bradshaw, Mark Fitzwilliams and Anthony Lathe. Then, almost alone in the Norfolk firmament of parish life, it has had unchanged boundaries for fifty years, whereas many parishes have found themselves in different groupings every five or ten years or so, as clergy numbers have diminished.

A chief blessing has been a score or so of deeply committed lay men and women of vast loyalty, deep honesty, ongoing hard work, strong faith and generous instincts, who have led the local congregations, while being at the same time enthusiastic about the Group. No names, no pack drill. But I do find it a bit alarming, twenty-two years after I left the Rectory, that in many cases it is still those same names leading the lay team.

Institutions need structure, and the structure of Anglican clergy teams is a weak thing, easily wrecked by a heedless rector or vicar (or by a careless appointment by the patrons). But here there is the valuable subsidiary structure of the Group Council and its committees, and the strength of monthly joint worship, neither of which we had at the Dereham Association. One very valuable aspect of team ministry is continuity. In single parishes, every time there is a change of priest there are months of interregnum; a new man or woman arrives and begins almost from scratch. But where there is a team there is no interregnum and the new rector or vicar joins an ongoing cruise, a much more holistic idea.

The future cannot be the same. The Hempnall Group began with a team of three full-time priests, supported by a succession of retired priests living in the villages. For a while we had Colin Way as a non-stipendiary priest (so we had to have clergy breakfasts on Saturdays as well as on Mondays). And then for a while we were four—Stuart, Colin, Keith and I. But now you have one and a half. Stuart and I always said that our chief task was to prepare the Group for the time when there would be just one full-time priest. That cannot now be long delayed. And that one priest will not have the joy and support and mutual knowledge that comes from a team of professional full-time colleagues.

So my own experience leads me to hope that real vibrant teams will be set up over wider areas as numbers of full-time leaders reduce. Why not an East Depwade team? Or a Stratton Association of Parishes? The Hempnall Group will have vast riches of experience to contribute.

* * *

What I have written here is a very clergy-centric account of my own experience of church life in groups and teams. Since leaving Hempnall I have become a Quaker. British Quakers do not have clergy, so I know that a great church can live without them (Quakers rather smugly like to say that they have no laity; every single Quaker is a minister). But these two churches are different animals. The Church of England needs its clergy, and I know from experience that they do much better in teams.

Shelton church

Peter Moss was born in Leicestershire. He served as a deacon and priest from 1961 until 1989 in County Durham and Norfolk. He resigned from the ministry in 1989 (for doctrinal reasons) and joined the Quakers, and worked for several years as a CAB volunteer. In 1959 he met Gonnie in a Mennonite Ecumenical work camp in Friesland—they celebrated 50 years of marriage in 2013. Gonnie worked in Hempnall Post Office with Mrs Gray. Peter and Gonnie have lived since 1990 in Foulsham, near Fakenham. Peter's 80th birthday falls on the same day as the fiftieth anniversary of the Group.

Occupation? Theologian!

Keith James

The heart attack occurred half way through my two-year course at Salisbury and Wells Theological College. It was the end of my first year, June 1986.

The previous two weeks I had been on 'placement', following in the footsteps of the rector and vicar at Thetford. They prayed, attended meetings, took services, made pastoral visits, did the paperwork, read, wrote sermons, preached, answered their correspondence, prepared for a hundred and one future events and even held an 'away-day' to discuss the shape of future ministry. Thetford had expanded rapidly as an overflow from the crowded east end of London, and this had now provoked serious problems: unemployment and disillusionment faced the children of those earlier incomers.

It was a Saturday—a day off at home, with the prospect of a farewell service the following day at Thetford as my placement came to an end.

I did not make it.

Instead I spent ten days in the Norfolk and Norwich hospital followed by a further ten days a couple of weeks later, and then convalescence at home until October. I returned to college and began again. But first I had to see my local doctor in Salisbury.

Dr Jeffrey Easton had a form to fill in. 'What,' he asked, 'is your occupation?'

'Student' seemed a bit lame for a man approaching fifty, and who would understand what an 'ordinand' (trainee priest) was? 'I know,' said Jeffrey, 'we'll put down *theologian*'.

I would never have thought of myself as a theologian.

A married man with four grown-up children, I had worked for twenty-two years as a dental hygienist, which had given me quite a high standard of living, enabling me to indulge my passion for cars and to buy a nice four-bedroom detached house with a large garden. Not the sort of academic, book-filled path you might have expected for a 'theologian'.

It is true that the last six years of all of that had also been a gentle realisation that something—someone?—God?—was calling me in a different direction.

Brought up in the Congregational church, I had left the church behind as I got married; we had our family, and got on with our lives. Baptisms, funerals, weddings, Easter and Christmas and the children going to Sunday School at our local Anglican Church in Tasburgh kept alive some sort of spiritual awareness.

For a time I would drop Ginny, my wife, off at the Sunday morning services, and then I drifted into going to services myself.

It was probably some two years later that our rector, Oswald Glass, retired. So we were in an interregnum, and by this time I was a churchwarden as well as the one who went up at six in the morning to start the very old and unreliable boiler every Sunday.

On this particular day the eight o'clock communion service was to be taken by the then rural dean, Cedric Bradbury, rector of the Hempnall Group. As I locked the vestry door behind him after the service he turned to me and said 'Have you ever thought of LOM?'

Not wanting to show my ignorance I probably mumbled 'no' and nothing more was said.

LOM: Local Ordained Ministry

The seed was sown. I didn't know it, but I was to become a 'theologian'.

First came the Reader's course. Various interviews, the usual C of E delays, and then acceptance to two years of part-time study; I had not written an essay for twenty years and more, nor learnt to read in any critical depth, but slowly it came together. The course was challenging. Challenging to what little faltering faith one had, as the two brilliant lecturers filled us with a mixture of doubt and certainty in equal measure. We were some twenty students of many different backgrounds, ages and belief. What a glorious mixture this church of ours can enfold as Christians! Sadly, some fell by the wayside as their sincere but simplistic ideas were crushed, but for me the experience taught me that faith and doubt are complementary bedfellows, and that the first can be strengthened by and indeed needs the other for a rich understanding of the mind of God.

Before the course finished I had somehow made the next step, attended further interviews, a selection conference at Ely, and been accepted for training as a priest in the Anglican Church. Next, to find a college that would have me!

The Bishop wanted me to go to an evangelical college in Cambridge; I was offered a place. But I also had an interview for Salisbury and Wells; I well remember the look on the principal's face when Ginny said she would not be coming with me. Unheard of! I was offered a place. I wrote a letter of acceptance to Cambridge as my Bishop wanted, only to receive a charming letter back to say that while the offer still stood I should in fact go to Salisbury! God moves in mysterious ways, and He knew that I was not cut out to spread the gospel in a Beach Mission on Felixstowe beach.

One obstacle remained. It is one thing for a man (or woman) to follow a calling from God, but it is *their* calling, and not their partner's. Ginny had been very supportive all along the way, but was it fair for her to give up our family home and that dream kitchen that she had just bought with her own earnings and had me install, or the garden that was to be her passion?

We stood looking out of the French windows onto the emerging garden that Ginny was creating from a field of clay. Could I, should I, ask such sacrifice?

When Ginny turned to me and said, 'It's only a house.' I knew I could go.

Fortunately the Diocese which had said I must be self-funding, changed its mind, and paid my fees and a living allowance. My eldest daughter and her husband moved down from London to live with Ginny, who was still working as a hygienist while I was at college, and so we were able to keep up the mortgage and keep the house.

But yes, I did shed a few tears as I drove away from Tasburgh in September 1985.

Two years of theological college

What did I learn?

I began to learn who I was. I read recently in a novel the description of a Florentine monk: 'for a holy man he was a complex mix of arrogance and humility'.

That was—and maybe still is—a fair description of me.

But the first thing I learnt at college was that my past 'achievements' counted for nothing. No one was interested in the fact that I had the best car in the car park, or that I had been earning very good money. I soon learnt how some of my fellow ordinands had had to sell even their modest houses, had moved with their families into cramped and dingy flats, tearing their children away from friends and school and their wives from their careers. I was fortunate, but it was not the sort of thing to brag about.

Again I learnt what a diverse church we are, for in my group of eleven students there was one fellow holier than the Pope and another so 'low church' he found it difficult to wear a cassock, let alone a stole. And among the women students I found that those who would have been quite content to remain deacons (this was prior to the vote enabling women to be ordained) would go on to be wonderful compassionate priests, while those who stridently craved to be made priests seemed to be the most unworthy of that great calling.

I learnt to write essays long into the night, literally cutting and pasting paragraphs on the floor of my room—no one had a computer in those dark ages! I learnt where to look for material, to read the first and last paragraph of chapters to gain the essence of a book, to put words together.

I learnt to see the beauty of poetry, the importance of paintings as food for the soul, and art, as expressions of worship.

I experienced all forms of services, and learnt the value of silence in worship.

In two years I learnt the Greek alphabet and the Hebrew alphabet—but nothing more.

I had travelled the roads with Jesus, begun to understand his teaching, had sat alongside the psalmist as he spoke to God of the human condition with all its joys and sorrows, gone into battle with the inhabitants of the Old Testament, and shared the anguish of Job.

And I had preached one, yes, just one, sermon.

And then I came to Hempnall. To be a 'theologian'.

The learning really was about to begin.

But what is theology? What does it mean to be a 'theologian'?

Towards the end of my college days my group had held a discussion. For all our differences, what did we honestly believe? We came up with only one thing we all agreed on. We all believed in God.

But what sort of God? That is where theology comes in.

The dictionary definition of a theologian is 'a person who engages in or is an expert in theology', which, again by definition, is 'the study of the nature of God'.

I am no expert—far from it—but it is that 'study of the nature of God' that I believe enables not only those called to ordination but all those who follow in Christ's footsteps to live out the life to which we are called, a life in the service of God and our fellow human beings.

And I believe that it is in part through the study of our fellow human beings that we begin to see 'the nature of God', what God is like.

It was through the people of the Hempnall Group that my future ministry was shaped and moulded, and I shall always be grateful to God for that.

I came as a 'curate'. In the Holy Communion Service of the *Book of Common Prayer* we pray for all 'Bishops and Curates, that they may both by their life and doctrine set forth thy true and lively word, and rightly and duly administer thy holy Sacraments.' No mention of rectors or vicars, but a reminder perhaps that *all* who are ordained have a 'cure' or care of souls, from the Latin *curatus*, care.

The primary role of a curate is not simply to be an assistant to the clergy already in post but to learn from them how to put into practice what has been learnt at theological college in such a way that the care—spiritual, mental and physical—of everyone in the parish, those of faith and those with none, is the underlying concern in all that is done in the name of Christ.

Nowhere, I feel, has this been more succinctly expressed than in the opening lines of a modern hymn:

> Brother, sister, let me serve you, let me be as Christ to you;
> Pray that I may have the grace to let you be my servant, too.

Some time after I had left Hempnall I was asked by the Bishop to conduct a survey of my fellow curates as to their experience in that first appointment in the Church. How well had that balance between 'assistant to the clergy' and 'one in need of nurture and teaching in the cure of souls' been achieved? Sadly some felt they had been used as a dogsbody, others left to flounder on their own. How fortunate I had been to come to Hempnall where, looking back, the balance had been so right.

What does a newly ordained curate need?

Perhaps the first requirement is respect. An acknowledgement of not only who they are but what they bring with them. Too often in the survey referred to above curates complained that their previous experience in their careers was overlooked, such skills as they might have acquired had gone unused, along with any special talents, such as a gift for music or art.

Peter Moss, the team rector, and I respected one another. I saw in him a man of great spirituality, with a wealth of expertise in church matters and great ability in the leadership of the Group: he was a source of knowledge that I had yet to learn.

I wonder what he saw in me? From the very beginning he treated me as an equal, a friend. And few though my gifts are he recognised, I think, that I had brought with me some 'earthiness', some ways of looking at the world and in particular at people from a perhaps more 'worldly' perspective. I remember that when I suggested to him that not everyone wanted to attend yet another meeting on a Friday evening after a week's work, or that evening meetings in general should end by ten o'clock at the very latest he was rather taken aback!

A second requirement is discipline.

Peter taught me discipline in that we met with the team vicar, Stuart Nairn, each morning for Morning Prayer in each of the parish churches in turn. I remember for instance sitting in the sun outside Fritton church, or the bitter cold of Bedingham in winter, but each one was a place where one could pray for the individuals of that particular parish. This was a practice that stayed with me when I left Hempnall, and seemed to be at the very heart of what ministry is about. Prayer for the people among the people.

Discipline too in personal devotions, in the time given to preparation for meetings, for services, for a daily routine that ensured a balance as far as possible between being in the study in the morning and out and about in the afternoon. And not least a discipline in having a proper day off each week, and time for leisure and relaxation.

But Peter also taught me the value of reading. During my training to be a Reader, the rector of Long Stratton, Bill Cummings, had advised me to preach 'with the Bible in one hand and a newspaper in the other'. Peter would have me use three hands, and in the third hold a copy of the latest novel I was reading or poet I had discovered. So my sermons and my preaching began to be formed.

A third requirement was a sense of humour, and of the ridiculous too! Many will remember the Harvest Supper after which all the clergy had to 'do a turn'—and the year we three did 'The Owl and the Pussy Cat' complete with a very pregnant cat and a huge runcible spoon. There is a need too to be able to laugh at oneself, and not become too serious-minded.

Fourth comes the purely practical: funerals, weddings, baptisms and how to handle them. Each one unique, each one requiring proper preparation, sensitive handling of all involved, and both a willingness to comply with people's wishes and a certain restraining influence to keep within the ethos that all are holy times in holy places. They are too a chance to preach with sensitivity, knowing that the congregation is made up of many shades of belief or none.

It is here that the essence of 'rural' ministry is most felt, as often whole communities are involved, whereas this feeling can be lost in the city. What a privilege it is for clergy to be so involved in such personal events in people's lives.

Then there is freedom. Freedom to visit people, freedom to begin a service for mothers and toddlers on a weekday afternoon, and to take Holy Communion to the residents at The Hollies care home once a month. Freedom to make hospital visits, and to take the sacrament to the housebound. Freedom to begin to spread my wings, to use and show the love of God just by being alongside people.

Finally there is the nitty-gritty of church life, the administration, the nuts and bolts that secure the finances, the maintenance of the buildings, the adherence to rules and regulations. Here in the Hempnall Group I found a framework of committees, parochial church councils, and the Group Council all working for the good of the whole while maintaining the individuality of each of the eight parishes. It was among those who served in so many ways, from cleaners to flower arrangers to treasurers and secretaries and that myriad of supporters who go about caring for this old and creaking Church of England that I learnt something of what it is to be a 'theologian'.

I was grateful to have their support when—I was still a curate, but by now ordained priest—first the non-stipendiary minister, Colin

Way, and then the rector and finally team vicar, Stuart, left the Group, and left me, along with one retired cleric, Kenneth Gray, to cope alone.

I can't quite recall how long my extended curacy was; I know that when I came I had expected it to last two years, but it was four and a half before I left, and I suppose I had been 'holding the fort' alone for at least some eighteen months before leaving the Group.

I was asked, unofficially I am sure, by the Archdeacon if I would consider staying on as team vicar when a new incumbent was appointed. But no, I felt it would have been unfair to the new rector, I had my feet too firmly under the table. Besides, I had learnt another thing about myself, which I am ashamed to admit: I am not a very good team player. I needed to be off on my own to pastures new, to take all I had learnt with me, and with the help and support of Ginny, to become the rector of seven small parishes in North Norfolk.

'For a holy man—a theologian—he was a complex mix of arrogance and humility.'

Sadly, some things never change. He still is.

Hardwick church

Keith James was born in Felixstowe and attended Felixstowe Grammar School. At 19, he joined the Royal Air Force and trained as a dental hygienist. While there he met and married Ginny, who was also training. On demob, he worked briefly for Westland Helicopters in Somerset and Birds Eye Foods in Lowestoft, and then joined a dental practice in Norwich where he worked for twenty-two years. He trained first as a Reader and then for ordination, studying at Salisbury and Wells Theological College. He was ordained deacon in 1987 to serve in the Hempnall Group, and priest in 1988; in 1991 he was appointed Rector of the Roughton Benefice of seven parishes in North Norfolk. From 1998 to 2001 he served as Vicar of Ascension Island in the South Atlantic and, on his return to the UK, as Chaplain to Laslett's Almshouses in Worcester. He retired from full-time ministry in 2004.

From Parishes to Group:

What was Happening Elsewhere?

Ernest Green

At first sight it seems it was a good idea to organise the pastoral care of England by dividing the country into convenient areas, putting a resident priest in charge of each one, and providing him with an income and housing. That was the theory behind the parish system in the Church of England. Unfortunately this approach has not stood the test of time. Adapting it to changing circumstances can be very slow, because, as it is an established church, any changes to the system can only come about after a tedious legislative process.

Sharing the clergy fairly among people who need their ministry has always been difficult. When I was training for ministry in the 1950s, Lincoln diocese was trying an experiment of grouping some country parishes around South Ormsby under the care of one rector assisted by curates. The rector came to talk at our theological college, but the only thing I remember him saying was that the clergy all had to have Public Service Vehicle licences, as they drove the parish bus to pick up parishioners for services. There is still a South Ormsby Group, although the number of churches (nine) is slightly fewer, and there is only one priest-in-charge. I don't know whether she has a PSV licence.

My first taste of parochial ministry was quite different, as a curate in a parish of 20,000. Lots of people meant lots of baptisms, weddings and funerals. One Sunday afternoon I baptised twenty-six babies in one service, and on the Saturday before the end of the income-tax year, weddings took place at forty-five-minute intervals, with congregations and brides entering by the West door and going out at the North door to avoid collisions. Towards the end of my curacy, the neighbouring parish down the hill was shrinking, as houses were being knocked down to make room for an extension to the steel mill. When its vicar retired the church closed, and we absorbed what was left of the parish, adding a population of 6,000 to ours. It was my first experience of pastoral reorganisation.

Ernest Green

After five years in non-parochial ministry I was instituted as vicar in a very different parish. It had two country churches within fifteen miles of Bristol, a city of half a million, but in a different diocese. Our diocese of Bath and Wells had over 600 parochial clergy, and being well endowed, did not have much trouble paying them. This was in sharp contrast to dioceses in the industrial areas of the North and Midlands, where there was a shortage of both clergy and endowments.

I arrived in that parish in 1965, a year after Bishop Launcelot Fleming had created the Hempnall Group and other similar groups in Norwich diocese. I don't remember news of his initiative reaching our diocese on the other side of the country. For us, pastoral reorganisation came from below. In 1970 the change to synodical government in the Church of England allowed resolutions from the grass roots (PCCs and Deaneries) to be debated in diocesan synod. Our rural dean was a Northerner with a social conscience, and despite opposition from the diocesan hierarchy, he managed to get the diocesan synod to pass a motion calling on the diocese to appoint a Pastoral Commission. This would consider the pastoral needs of the diocese with a view to reducing drastically, perhaps by half, the number of clergy employed in its parishes. I found myself one of the six clergy appointed to this Commission of twelve. It was hard work, not just in the number of meetings, but also in visiting deanery synods and parishes to explain and commend the proposals.

I no longer have the final report of the Commission to hand for reference, but I remember trying to digest lots of statistics, discussing the merits of team and group ministries, and agonising over the problem of moving clergy who in those days had the right to stay in their parishes for life, with no compulsory retirement age. (The Chairman, a gentle and scholarly archdeacon, was heard to murmur 'Of course, in the old days they used to poison their chalices'.) We produced a substantial report which ended with some fairly simple rules of thumb. Each deanery would have a number of clergy allocated to it, roughly based on its population figures; in towns, one priest for 10,000 people, and one for 5,000 in the country. These were permanent, incumbent posts; curates were a bonus, as theirs were short-term appointments. It was left to the deanery, having considered the report, to decide how its allocation should be deployed. Any plan a deanery made would have to be implemented gradually as clergy moved or retired.

Bath and Wells diocese had been making piecemeal attempts at pastoral reorganisation for some years before this. I came to a parish (Churchill) which had been formed from parts of two others immediately before my arrival. Sandford had been taken from Winscombe parish and put with Churchill, while Langford had been taken from Churchill parish to join with Burrington parish. Although I had only one PCC, the two churches took time to feel part of one parish, as they kept separate accounts. In due course the Pastoral Commission's plan affected my own parish, as when my neighbour retired in 1978 his parish was joined with mine and the Green family moved down the road to the parsonage he had vacated. So I had in my care four churches: Churchill, Sandford, Burrington and Langford.

I give this background to contrast the coming together of my parishes with those in the Hempnall Group. Comparing my parishes in Somerset with the Hempnall Group, I see how fortunate the Group was that Bishop Launcelot was able to put together three clergy of the calibre of Peter Bradshaw, Anthony Lathe and Mark Fitzwilliams to minister to a population of about 2,500. This was a far cry from the levels of staffing Bath and Wells were proposing ten years later (or that I had known as a curate!). It was inevitable that a team of three clergy in the Hempnall Group would not be maintained for long. When I arrived in 1991 Keith James, who had come in 1987 as a curate in training, had been the only ordained member of staff for eighteen months. He left later in the year for his first incumbency. In 1992 Conal Mahony came to fill the vacant team vicar post, and in 1993 we were joined by Michael Windridge as a curate in training. Dorothy, my wife, was already a deacon when we arrived, but became a full-time carer for her mother in our first year at Hempnall. When her mother needed extra care and moved to London, Dorothy was able to give help as an honorary curate. So by 1994, when she was one of the first women ordained priest in Norwich Diocese, we had four priests in the team, which was two more than our normal strength; a bonus we could not plan to rely on. Dorothy, who at our wedding had promised to obey me, was sent off to cover for sickness, holidays and vacancies in other parishes in the deanery. In her first year as a priest she learnt how to conduct the communion service in twenty-one different churches.

Team ministries, in which two or more clergy of incumbent status work together, can be of great benefit to both the clergy and their congregations. First, the clergy have support and fellowship from others in their own profession. In eleven years as a rural dean in two different dioceses I have seen the loneliness sometimes experienced by clergy working on their own, with no one to turn to for help or advice. Secondly, members of a clergy team are likely to have differing skills and qualities which enhance, not only each other's ministries, but the life of their congregations as well. Hempnall was the only time I worked in a team ministry, and to work with Conal was enriching, supportive and fun.

This is not to say that team ministries are the answer to all problems of providing for the care of parishes. If the clergy are to be allocated even-handedly among the population of the country, then team ministries will be based in towns, where the larger populations are. In Bath and Wells diocese the teams that have been set up are generally centred on a town, but include some surrounding rural parishes, for example in Wellington, Ilminster and Yeovil. There is one team (Marlbrook) within Bath itself. In other dioceses too the team ministries are normally in urban areas.

Another drawback to team ministry is that the clergy are not trained to work in teams, and many have gone into the ministry because they have expectations of working independently when they have charge of a parish. I don't know whether this will ever be seriously addressed in selecting and training candidates for ministry. Related to this is the matter of changes in the make-up of the team, when a team member leaves and has to be replaced. Will relationships with the new team work as well as they did before the change? Stuart Nairn raised this question in the Group's twenty-first anniversary publication, and it still needs to be considered by patronage boards.

A team ministry affects not just the clergy, but their congregations as well. People start to worship together and meet each other across parish boundaries. The separate PCCs come together to exchange ideas and plan action for the whole group in a group or team council. This had not happened in Churchill for a number of reasons. First, the churches at Sandford and Langford had never been parish churches, and felt insecure through being moved from one mother church to another. To some degree I became their only security. At the end of a meeting at Sandford to talk about the proposed coming together with Burrington an influential lady in the congregation said 'I don't mind who we are joined with as long as Mr Green is our vicar.' (Better the devil you know!) The scheme of reorganisation was simply envisaged as putting two parishes in the care of the same incumbent; saving a man, in other words (and in those days they were all men!). The four congregations were fairly self-sufficient; three had choirs and there were three Mothers' Union branches, apart from other organisations. Then there were social factors. One PCC included the Lord Lieutenant and a number of high-flying professional people. They were not available to take part in parish life as much as those who worked in or near the parish. Again, although patronage was not really a factor on this occasion, it is interesting to note that one parish was unusual in that the patrons were the parishioners.

Although when the Hempnall Group was formed it had fewer clergy than its separate parishes had had before 1964, Peter Bradshaw was insistent that each member of his team had eight churches to look after and each church had three clergy. This must have had an invigorating effect on the congregations, giving them the feeling of belonging to a church that stretched beyond their own village. People began thinking of the Group and not the parish as being the more important component of the local church. Resources were pooled and skills were shared. Work with young people in the holiday club and the youth group was a possibility because it was a Group and not an individual parish undertaking. The Group choir could attempt more interesting music, as in the Christmas carol service, which became an annual fixture. Working as a Group not only offered more possibilities to the individual congregations, but it also enabled us to engage more effectively with the wider church. The visit of the Revd Ashoke Biswas (now Bishop of Kolkata) was a Group occasion which resulted in the formation of a link between Hempnall Group and a girls' school in Kolkata, where we were able to fund an improvement to their water supply. This was in addition to a lot of other giving to charities at home and overseas that was already going on.

This is not to say that everyone immediately switched from thinking parochially to thinking as a group. People get very attached to their local church building, and it is not just in the Hempnall Group that I have found parishioners absenting themselves from Sunday worship because it was not held in 'their' church. When I had a parish with only one church (such parishes still exist) I was left speechless by a parishioner who came back from holiday and told me she didn't go to church while away because she couldn't go to 'her' church; she would go to no other. Sometimes parochialism comes out subconsciously, as when someone announced at a Group meeting that a coming event was to take place at St Margaret's, completely forgetting that there are three churches dedicated to St Margaret in the Group. Again, there were those who were surprised that I was hurrying my after-church coffee because I needed to go on to take a service in another church in the Group. Peter Bradshaw had declared that each church would have three priests and each priest would have eight churches, but sometimes it seemed that only the clergy really appreciated the second clause of his maxim.

It may come as a surprise to people in the Hempnall Group to learn that elsewhere there are church congregations whose members do not have many skills to share in furthering the work of the church. In some large housing estate parishes, vicars have to scratch around to find people willing and able to fill the basic jobs of secretary and treasurer for the parochial church council. In a different situation again are country villages that are 'dormitories' for city workers who commute long distances to work each day, or where a lot of cottages are second homes for town dwellers, and empty during the week. Fortunately the Hempnall Group, although it is small in population, has a high proportion of church members who have both skills and time which they offer generously to the church. I remember gratefully the work of members of the ministry team, the buildings officers, musicians, youth helpers, news sheet distributors and many others, besides those who filled the statutory offices of churchwarden, secretary and treasurer. Many years ago a Bishop of Bath and Wells visited a small parish in the south of his diocese to explain to them that when their vicar retired they would be looked after by the vicar of the neighbouring parish. He was taken by surprise during the questions after his talk when someone asked, 'But if our vicar's living in the next village, who's going to put out the tables for the whist drive?'

When Peter Dawson was Archdeacon (1977–1993) he initiated a series of occasional meetings for clergy working in multiple cures. It provided a forum for the sharing of information; some clergy asked for suggestions to solve problems they had encountered, others told of ideas that had worked in their parishes. Coming back from one of these meetings Conal (or was it Keith?) and I remarked to each other that a lot of problems which other groups of parishes faced were problems which had not arisen in the Hempnall Group. The Group had worked well from the beginning. The parishes had knit together under a good team of clergy, and the cooperation engendered among the laity had become self-perpetuating. No doubt some of this was due in the first place to Peter Bradshaw's personality, but the enduring life of the Group has depended chiefly on the laity who caught his vision of what the church in the countryside could be, and passed that vision on to others. After half a century the Church is still looking for new patterns of pastoral care, but the Hempnall Group continues. It seems an appropriate moment to invoke the words of Dag Hammarskjold: 'For all that has been, thanks. To all that shall be, yes.'

Shelton church

After National Service (RAF), Cambridge and theological college, Ernest was ordained to a curacy in Yorkshire. He then worked with students and on the staff of a cathedral before returning to parish ministry in North Somerset. After seventeen years there he moved to a town parish on the Isle of Wight. Having served as a rural dean in two dioceses for a total of eleven years, he was glad to find that Depwade deanery did not need a rural dean when he came to Hempnall in 1991.

Living Communities

Conal Mahony

Once upon a time, when I was a Franciscan friar teaching theology, I noticed that with one or two slight adjustments to the year's programme I could be free of teaching commitments for two terms. With the agreement of my superiors I enrolled on a course, 'Human Relations for the Pastoral Ministry', run by the Richmond Fellowship in London. This offered the opportunity to spend half of each week living, helping and sharing in their therapeutic communities of people who had suffered emotional or mental problems; the rest of the week was spent in college studying sociology and psychology, with weekly sessions of group dynamics, and seminars where we were able to share reflections on what we were learning and discovering, and on how it might affect our lives and work. Towards the end of the course we were each expected to present a paper. Mine was entitled 'From Institution to Community' in which I attempted to apply some of the principles and practices we had experienced to the living-out of the community life of the friary. It seemed important that there should be a closer sharing of ideals and aspirations, deeper interpersonal relations and shared prayer in a less formal setting, as well as a full liturgical life.

Returning to my community, the student house of the Province in the seclusion of the beautiful Constable countryside, I was able to contribute to the process of change which was taking place there. A major decision was to spend time in smaller units as well as in the larger community and thus to experience the benefits of more intimate relationships as well as the strengths and opportunities that the full community offered. Soon we were to move from Suffolk to establish the Franciscan Study Centre in Canterbury and there we enshrined in the buildings the new form of life. Instead of one large friary to house forty to fifty members, we built and lived in three separate houses while still also forming the one larger community. Thus we were able to experience the closeness of the few and the richness of the larger community in all that its life had to offer.

Several years later, after a circuitous journey, I arrived in the Hempnall Group and was excited by what I found. Here were eight villages, the basic sociological entity, each preserving its more intimate life, but brought together by an administrative decision to form a group whose life and ethos surpassed a mere institution and had become a genuine community with a sharing of ideals, resources, skills, relationships and, most important of all, worship. The life and spirit of the Group had been fostered and enriched by the gifts and contribution of dedicated clergy and lay people working closely together from the very beginning and down through the developing years. It has been always important that the clergy relate appropriately in the Christian community in which they are called to serve, to minister, not to boss. Their task is to facilitate and enable the laity to exercise their rightful ministry in all its varied forms, both in the individual parish and in the Group.

One of the greatest values of the Group is that it can draw on the skills and the experience of the people from across all the parishes. To this end, the establishing of all the mission teams, which focused on worship, learning and growing, wholeness, young people, pastoral, finance, outreach, social events, and marriage preparation—originally drawing on a membership of seventy across the whole Group—was most important to ensure the fulfilment of the Group's task while avoiding any feeling of elitism. All these were in addition to the incredible number of people who help in different ways, caring for buildings, churchyards, and local people in each of the several villages. There has been encouragement throughout the Group's history for members to own and belong to their small village church community and to the wider Group. This was greatly enhanced by the decision of the original three clergy not to divide responsibility for the villages between them, but to work on the principle that each parish had three clergy, and each clergy person had eight villages in his care. The fact that in 2014 the Hempnall Group of Parishes is celebrating fifty years of continued and continuing existence owes much to that early organisational principle which has been applied throughout its life.

Some of the parishes have been better endowed historically than others and the Group has enabled a sharing of financial resources, for example, in meeting the cost of ministry, as happened in some of the primitive communities in the early life of the Christian Church.

Despite financial constraints becoming ever more difficult, both the individual parishes and the Group have endeavoured to be very outward-looking to the concerns and needs of the wider society of the nation and world. Individual parishes have tried to maintain the support of their chosen charities, while the Group has always responded financially very generously to the mission projects it has sponsored, to annual appeals and especially to disasters and emergencies as they arise. It has also responded by holding special services and vigils on such occasions. This has all helped to prevent parish and group communities turning in on themselves; rather, it has encouraged the view that they are all part of a wider network of human existence, relationships and need.

Lest this all begins to sound too serious and solemn, one of the great strengths of the Group has been a sense of adventure and fun, which have greatly fostered its togetherness. Into this bracket fall away-days together, weekends at Massingham and Ditchingham, pilgrimage holidays to Iona, Assisi (twice), Lindisfarne, and Parceval Hall in Yorkshire, as well as lunches and parties to celebrate regular events such as Harvest and all special occasions. While the parishes also enjoy their social life, these larger events would not have been possible without the real spirit of togetherness of the wider Group.

Surely, the most definitive activity of any Christian community is its life of worship and prayer. While attempting to be available to all traditions, the Hempnall Group has largely preserved a liberal catholic attitude in its witness and sacramental worship. Individual parishes have gathered for worship in their parish churches but there has been a long tradition of shared worship in the Group with services, usually the Eucharist, involving the wider community. These have been organised on a basis of visiting each of the parish churches in turn thus enabling a fuller, more varied and at times experimental liturgy to be experienced. Similarly, happenings such as Advent and Lent series of seasonal reflective services have been regularly organised on a rotational basis, as at times has a Group celebration of Morning and Evening prayer.

I believe that there flows both into the worship and out of the worship a deep sense of caring for one another and the world in which we live. This is manifest in all sorts of ways in the local villages and across the parish boundaries. I would not hesitate to say that the Group is founded on and well expresses true Christian love. However,

I would not want to give the impression that there is no tension. As I have said at another time, the only place where people exist side by side without tension is in our churchyards. The mark of a real and vibrant community is that it expresses care and concern, is founded on and maintained by love, and is energised by tension and difference.

No Christian community exists for its own sake. It is there in its time and place to serve and to give witness to the society of which it is part and so build the Kingdom of God on earth. I believe that it can only fulfil this task if it truly reflects something of the intimate love-life of the Trinity which is God, who in turn chose to be united intimately with human beings through the Incarnation, and Jesus in turn chose a dozen apostles and a wider group of seventy disciples to continue His work. A living and lively relationship between the smaller unit and a larger group is a very apt model for the church at large in its mission to achieve God's purpose. It means that the church can be, and can be experienced as, a real community and not just an institution. This is why I was excited when I came to the Hempnall Group, and why I am deeply thankful that I was allowed to live and minister in its midst until my retirement. Even now, living outside its boundaries as required, I and my wife are welcomed back to the Group and all of the parishes to share its life, its worship and its love.

Woodton church

Conal Mahony was born in Bristol. He trained as a Roman Catholic Franciscan friar and priest, teaching moral theology and working as an accredited counsellor. He joined the Church of England in 1984; after running a psychiatric day centre, and while director of an ecumenical family care centre, he was licensed as a non-stipendiary priest. He moved, with his wife Jackie and their children Catherine and Martin, to the Hempnall Group when he was appointed curate in 1992. He subsequently served as team vicar and was then team rector from 1997 until he retired in 2008.

The Hempnall Group: The Laity (1)

George Levack

The Levack family came to Fritton in 1973. George continued as Bursar at New Hall, Cambridge, until October. Meanwhile Patricia had been supervising building work while he became a weekend visitor. George had visited Morningthorpe Manor shortly after the war, driving from Norwich with his mother who knew Mrs Sargent from Red Cross days, and Carole Sargent similarly.

We returned to Norfolk after many years abroad so that we could be near to Meadow Cottage in Overstrand, where our younger son was cared for under the banner of Elizabeth Fitzroy homes, a most admirable organisation for cases requiring nursing care. We had not in fact intended to live south of Norwich, but having exhausted ourselves and all the houses near Overstrand on the market at that time, we saw an advertisement for Old Hall, Fritton, a house that we quickly came to love. It had the advantages of a quiet and a delightful position on the common; and for a family back from Africa it was all that we could wish for from a house in England.

We quickly established links with the Hempnall Group of Parishes: the Rector, Jeffery Smith, had incidentally been a missionary in Africa. Patricia, a Roman Catholic, became a loyal parishioner of St Edmunds Church in Bungay, where the priest-in-charge was appointed traditionally from the Benedictine Abbey of Downside in Somerset.

The Hempnall Group, it will be recalled, was sponsored by Bishop Launcelot Fleming and brought into adolescence by Peter Bradshaw and Cedric Bradbury with the almost mythical assistance of Mark Fitzwilliams and Anthony Lathe. Its main problem was the size of its area (six parishes, eight churches) and the small size of its congregations. Although one of its parishes, Hempnall, was clearly the largest and most populous, it was essential that there should be one leader and one or two clergy to coordinate an active agricultural organism. Initially this had been effected by having the rector's house at Morningthorpe, part of almost the smallest parish (though with two churches). But in due course, by 1983, the Rectory was set up in Hempnall as the geographical centre of the area.

It is true to say that the regrouping itself led to difficulty: the need was to be sensitive to the smaller parishes while achieving clear direction for the whole community. Without much knowledge of the original scheme I became (as a subsequent member of the ministry team to Michael Sargent) associated with Peter Moss, himself appointed to follow Jeffery Smith as the Group's rector. The team represented each of the six parishes, together with Peter Moss, Stuart Nairn and Colin Way. We held regular meetings and, it seemed to me, placed particular emphasis on the fact that membership of the team should by design and practice support the work of the clergy, taking even some of the load resulting from the decision, as far as possible, to hold regular services in the six parishes each Sunday. Our meetings also drew strength from the thoughtful study of various problems of the church generally and from connections with other trains of thought and worship in other parts of Norfolk. We supported the idea of Group services each month in one or other of our churches, ideally to be attended by parishioners of the several churches that composed the Group. I have never reconciled this belief with the diminishing attendance by members of all six parishes at the one monthly Group service. It is an opportunity lost that more people do not attend these services.

With the regrettable resignation by Peter Moss of his leadership of the Group, there was a reworking of the group ministry concept. Under his successors, Ernest Green and Conal Mahony, the Group coordination took on a different shape: regular meetings, not of representatives of the parishes, but of the various working committees for Group activities. These looked after worship, social activities, children and youth work, learning and growing, outreach, and finance, so that inter-parish planning and discussion began to happen at this level. In my view this is an added centralisation of the system but one that has not reduced the level of parish activity. Conal and Liz Billett (the team vicar) produced a widely admired example of group continuity; and they could not have given a better leadership for a functioning real life of our church in a developing district.

George Levack

George Levack was born in India, now Pakistan. He went to school in Norwich and Edinburgh and then to Oxford university. He worked for the colonial service abroad, in Palestine, Gold Coast/Ghana, N. Rhodesia/Zambia and then in various posts in this country. He is married to Patricia. After his retirement they moved to Fritton in South Norfolk, where they lived for twenty-seven years. They have now moved to Sandford near Weston–Super-Mare.

Fritton church

The Hempnall Group: The Laity (2)

Enid Gray

Enid wrote her contribution to this collection not many months before the end of her full and well-lived life.

Eight churches: all very different buildings and congregations but happily melded together into the Hempnall Group. When that happened we were living in Somerset. My husband and I retired at the same time. We had to leave our house and expended much energy looking for another one, preferably in Norfolk where I was born and spent my schooldays. At the secondary school where I was teaching I was looking after a young teacher who was waiting to be interviewed by the headmistress. I asked about her background and, *mirabile dictu*, found that I had been at Norwich High School with her mother! Her brother lived in Woodton, he needed to sell his house; were we interested? We went to see. Into the sitting room we went. My husband, a keen gardener, looked out of the window at the garden and said, 'We'll have it.'

That is how we landed in the Hempnall Group, to our benefit. We went to the church AGM at which there was so much laughter that we realised we were in the right place. Think of it, that meant that in time we had friends in eight villages. Among them was a succession of clergy who provided leadership and their individual gifts. We loved them, they loved their people. I meditate on the symbolism of the foot-washing on Maundy Thursday.

I go back to the days when the clergy did everything. In the Hempnall Group we rejoice in lay participation. The laity act as deacons, take the prayers, read the lessons, take Holy Communion to the housebound. Just as important in the functioning of the Group are the contributions of the ministry teams. Each of these has members from all the parishes. The worship team is obviously concerned with the actual services; the learning and growing team is a think tank for the future, it organises informative talks, discussion groups, outings and visits to places such as Lindisfarne and King's College, Cambridge; the outreach team concentrates on matters of interest and importance where the church can give support and help—for example, collecting tools that will enable people in Africa to get a job;

the youth team looks at ways of responding to the needs of young people. There is also a team to consider finance, consisting of each parish treasurer and the Group treasurer; and a social team which provides hospitality and organises the catering for Group events. In all these things women are as active as men and, praise be, this includes the clergy.

But we are not turned in on ourselves, far from it. We support Christian Aid, a hospital in Africa, the Vidiyal Trust and a number of charities. Until recently we have also been associated with a secondary school for girls in Calcutta. One can only marvel at the generosity of so many people.

In these difficult times there is so much goodness and kindness—that's the Hempnall Group. And much prayer. 'Open my eyes to beauty, open my mind to wonder, my ears to others and my heart to You.'

Bedingham church

My mother, Enid Gray, so enjoyed returning to Norfolk in retirement, the county of her birth and of her Norwich High School days before going up to Oxford. She married Ken, a clergyman, after graduating in 1938, and they had three children, seven grandchildren and twelve great-grandchildren. Their twenty-three years together in Woodton before my father died in 1998 were full and joyous. Ken had initially just wished to retire to gardening and birdwatching, but he soon became involved taking services and helping with various interregnums in local parishes. Enid did likewise: she was immersed in the Group, in discussion groups, the WI, was always involved in local activities, and was a churchwarden for many years. If anything she had, at times, to be 'slowed down'! My parents were blessed with many very good kind friends and neighbours in the Group, which in turn enabled Enid to stay at Windwhistle. Her very active intelligent mind needed feeding and stimulating, and needed also to give and express love to her neighbour. In 2012 she reached the age of ninety-seven and resolved she had come to the end of her full and very happy years, thirty-seven of them in Woodton.

A Pocket Full of . . .

Liz Billett

The Hempnall Group is a very good place to be. In eleven years of living, loving, laughing and lamenting, I am a richer person.

Often the first thought when we begin something new is to say, 'what can I give?' or 'what can I do?'

It was no different for me. On the day of my licensing as team vicar in the Hempnall Group of Parishes in Hempnall church I had in my cassock pocket a handful of seeds. The seeds represented for me some of the things I thought I might be able to do and the gifts I might offer to give this Group. What I know now, eleven years later, is that rather than giving, I have received so much more, 'pockets full' of seeds if you like, wonderful gifts given to me and received from this special place and its people. While these gifts are particular and personal there is something here not just for me but for everyone. In them are underlying values that reflect the nature of this Group and what it says about the God they love and serve.

A pocket full of joy

The Group knows how to have fun. My first glimpse of this was on that first evening walking into Hempnall village hall—what a sight to behold! Stretching down the length of the building, a table decked with red and white checked table cloths, just visible under a mouth-watering array of scrumptious food. Out of the corner of my eye, I could see another table, this one with bottles of wines and juices. This feast was not going to run out of food—or wine! I remember thinking; this is not a rich tea and a cup of coffee group of parishes. How right I was! Whether as individual parishes or coming together as a Group, these good people know how to enjoy themselves. But it is more than just fun. It comes, I think, from a deep sense that life is good and to be enjoyed. Their faces, laughter, smiles and winks all say to those around them , who are sometimes newcomers as I was, 'Come and join in.' I did and I am still here.

There is a Jewish story of a man who died, and when he reached the gates of heaven God was there to meet him. He'd thought of all the things God might say to him, but he was surprised when all God said was, 'Well, did you enjoy my world then?'

Because of the Hempnall Group I have enjoyed God's world. There has been the delight of discovering new places together, such as Iona, Assisi, Lindisfarne, the Yorkshire Dales, and walks through familiar parish fields and lanes. There have been times shared simply and wonderfully in numerous other ways with God's good people.

Through the Group I have discovered more of a God who longs for us to enjoy life in all its fullness, and his world, in sunshine and in rain.

A pocket full of kindness and goodness

Life, though, is not always jolly and fun-filled. We know only too well that sharp unexpected winds, worry and care can blow us off our feet leaving us a bit bruised and battered. At such times, to find expressions of kindness and goodness is a true joy.

Where we meet such qualities, where each is inclined to the other in compassion, there, we can be sure, is God.

When the cold harsh winds of life have come my way, and sometimes blown me over, simple acts of kindness and care have been a balm, unconsciously given by the people of the Group, that has enabled me to get up on my feet again and continue. In and through them God has been present to me.

A pocket full of thankfulness

This sense of joy mixed with kindness and goodness spills over into thankfulness. It is no coincidence that the heart of the Group's worshipping life is the sharing of a meal; the Eucharist, which means Thanksgiving.

When we read the Scriptures we discover that something important always happens when food is shared, whether that be in inviting a stranger to come in to share a meal after a long journey, a barbeque on the beach or a meal out with those who some people would not put on their guest list! Food is more than food. We know this for ourselves: in meals shared with family and friends, the simple and the big celebrations, something happens. We cannot always put our finger on it, but in the talking and the sharing, in the sitting and the eating we find ourselves nourished.

In the Eucharist we celebrate and partake in God's life. We share a meal, sometimes round a table grandly decked with the best linen and silver, sometimes a picnic in the open air around a bale of straw with earthenware vessels; in sad and hard times as well as good and joyful times. And through all creation we receive the gift and blessing of God in bread and wine. In the Incarnation we remember his Son's life, broken and given for the sake of the world. In the words of the Eucharist we hear Jesus saying, 'Do this in remembrance of me', so we take him at his word, and we do just that. In the doing of this we find ourselves caught up in the life of God, sometimes in blessing, because that is our place in life at that moment and at other times, broken because that too can be where we are. In the blessing and the breaking, in the living and receiving, something is shared and we are thankful.

A pocket full of generosity

A life of joy lived kindly, and of thankfulness in good and sad times, is not to be kept to oneself but given away for the benefit of others.

This open-hearted generosity comes in many forms. One way in which the Group offers such generosity to many is symbolised by its always open churches. The opportunity to step inside these beautiful buildings for whatever reason, to find a holy yet homely and loved space, is something valued by many. People come finding churches not covered in dust sheets to protect or locked against the intruder who might upset things or take what is not 'ours'. They come finding a tangible atmosphere of devotion and peace through the prayer and presence of people in our own time and down through the generations. Those who step inside and leave their mark in the visitors books testify to this:

> 'We came in search of our roots and found peace and helping hands.'
>
> 'What a treasure of a church—even the lions are smiling.'
>
> 'My inner strength is developing…'
>
> 'Came to pray and just be so wonderfully peaceful.'

Such a space changes people.

In his book on Norfolk Churches David Stanford says,

> As well as places of deeply felt religious belief, these churches are beautiful historic statements of our heritage and each one offers the

> warmest of welcomes to all visitors. They are a credit to those who run the group and a clear vision of how things can be.

How right he is.

The Group also has a long and proud history of giving generously to local, national and international organisations and charities, regularly and in times of crisis. The commitment to this continues even in financially strained times. Such generosity comes from a thankful heart and is a blessing unbeknown to many.

A pocket full of faithfulness

This generous loving service to God's people and God's world is not sporadic but faithful. Day by day, week by week, month by month, year by year the faithfulness of many continues. Often unseen and unnoticed, people are drawn in to 'keep the rumour of God alive'. From the care of buildings and churchyards, cleaning, and making coffee, to stapling the magazine and organising social events, and in the ordinariness of everyday life.

The Group works through a variety of Mission Teams. These enable a greater number of people than a single ministry team would encompass to share their gifts and interests. These teams reflect something of what is important to the Group, and through them God's care and love for his world is made known.

The wise stewardship of all and the sharing of the resources we have been given is managed through the finance team; the longing for life in all its fullness for each person and all creation through the wholeness team; the desire for justice and peace locally and globally through the outreach team; the hope to share faith with children through the team recently refocused to care for families and young people; the need to deepen our delight and understanding through the learning and growing team, recently merged with the team caring for our offering of worship—the bedrock of our life together.

People and priest together are involved in the great enterprise of the triune God, that of creation and redemption. Our life flows from the life of God, where relationship is of the essence. Here in the triune God we discern integration of individuality and mutuality, there is no domineering spirit but mutual sacrificial loving, and the Group, in its way, seeks to flesh this out in the ways it lives.

Liz Billett

God asks us to be faithful, not successful. In a success-driven world faithfulness is sometimes hard to come by, but you can come by it here, in this group of parishes, in pocketfuls. To see and experience it is truly powerful and humbling. Faithfulness is present here and now because of the faithfulness of the past. We are all the people we are because of those who have gone before us; so this is where we find ourselves as we celebrate fifty years of the Hempnall Group of Parishes.

My pockets are full, because of the good people of the Hempnall Group. Through them I have received a greater joy and love of life, known real care and kindness, that has led to a deep sense of gratitude and thankfulness for their faithful generosity to me and many. Where we meet such qualities, there, we can be sure, is God.

Thank you, good people.

Topcroft church

Liz is the daughter of a West Norfolk farmer. She has spent much of her working life as a nurse and midwife. She now works as an Anglican priest in her home county in rural Norfolk. She enjoys anything creative, cooking, gardening, painting and walking. She has, with her husband Tony, worked to create a space in their home and garden for people who need to have space for themselves. She and her husband have two sons.

Reflections on the Hempnall Group of Churches

Michael Kingston

As winter gives way to spring, there are snowdrops poking through the ground in Hempnall churchyard, daffodils at Morningthorpe, and beautiful primroses at Topcroft. A summer day at Bedingham shows the splendour of the church standing next to the priory, and reveals the architectural grandeur of Shelton. Then there is Fritton, hidden in the trees, Hardwick with just half a tower, all that remains after the partial collapse following a storm in 1770. Finally there is Woodton with its distant connections with the Nelson family. Eight churches nestling in the South Norfolk countryside, bypassed by the traffic as it speeds down the A140 to Ipswich or winds down the B1332 to Bungay. These are all unique churches, just as the communities they serve are all different.

I'm a suburban lad who was brought up in the London Borough of Bromley and spent all his life living in suburbia until 2009. We wanted to move, but to stay in Norfolk. The prospect of caring for eight old buildings and communities was daunting. It is funny the things we look for when discerning the work of God. My wife, Maggie, enjoys playing tennis and her prayer was that there might be a tennis court in the village. Imagine her surprise and delight when that prayer was answered as we walked round the village hall in Hempnall. Not just a tennis court, but an active group who play regularly. As for me, I wanted to be part of a community whom I could love and help to grow in their faith, while at the same time getting to know the local community and share my love of God with them.

So as we prayed and came to interview, we thought this was a good place to be, and thankfully so did the interviewing group! My ministry started on a cold night in February 2009 when many from the villages came to see what the new rector looked like. In those early days the Ordnance Survey map was kept close just to find the churches. One of the first things to hit me was the number of people doing things. The church office was manned four mornings a week by a very competent secretary and administrator. It is amazing how much paper is created and communication seems so important with a group like this. Then I would be working with another part-time priest, Liz Billett. Liz, whose husband is the rector of Diss, works four days a week—one-and-a-half people doing what three people did fifty years ago. How would I cope, having been used to doing everything by myself? The answer is, very well. Liz and I complement each other, which is a benefit to the parishioners and myself.

How do you work out the service pattern?

A sample pattern of services over a month is shown at the back of this book. It is not easy, but we ensure that there is a service in each church at least once a month. Fritton and Shelton are used in the summer months only, because of the lack of power. Surprisingly it is not a mad dash around the countryside on a Sunday morning going between services. To start with the roads are really too narrow to go too fast! The clergy are helped by a number of helpers who set up the church, and act as readers and intercessors. There are lay deacons who actually help take the service. All this is a wonderful assistance and even if we arrive a few minutes late there is not a problem. Sometimes the small congregations are like a meeting of friends. The Anglican tradition of sitting at the back is put to one side as we meet, sometimes in the choir stalls. We have a Group service on the first Sunday in the month in different churches round the Group. This takes on a different dimension from a small group, and it is good for us all to get together and experience a full church—worship can feel very different, particularly the singing. It is also encouraging to the smaller congregations to see that they are part of something bigger. Maybe we all need to learn that? There may only be five or six people at a service, but that group is part of a vast worshipping community throughout the country and the world. To help us all, the rota showing services, helpers and readings is issued every four months and given out to over sixty people. Yes there are times when it is easy on a Sunday morning to forget the time or, on occasions, to head in the wrong direction, but the folk here are gracious in their understanding and we can only try to do our best.

Laughter seems to be a feature—maybe it's important not to take ourselves too seriously. Laughter comes from enjoying each other's company over a cup of coffee or a meal. The smell of bacon frying and hearing it sizzle in the pan after the Easter morning vigil was a wonderful extra. These folk enjoy each other's company. Often the chatting after the worship is longer than the service itself. Importantly, most people stay, which is all rather lovely.

What do I think I bring to this Group?

It is easy to try and be somebody we are not—we will soon fail and parishioners will see through us. It was important to be me—that is a change in itself, which would take time for the parishioners to come to terms with. I would most certainly do things differently from Conal, the previous incumbent. Part of the job of a new incumbent is to ease into the job—look, listen rather than change things. It takes time to build up a relationship, and when this is done, we can see what—if anything—needs to be looked at, and then tweak things. It's important *together* to seek God and what he wants us to do. I must say that the challenge of caring for eight medieval buildings is on the surface an impossible task, only to be carried out with the grace of God and the help of many. This raises the inevitable question: mission or maintenance? Perhaps both can go hand in hand. This Group has the great advantage that the churches are open all the time. The buildings are all well cared for. Repairs are carried out as needed, money permitting. What happens when the money runs out? We will tackle that hurdle when it arises. I suspect that the local community will be called on to assist. These places of worship belong to their communities, not just to the few who worship week by week.

So what has happened in that time?

I hope I have now eased myself into a new and challenging role and carried on with what has been going on for the time of the Group. We have held an annual party in the Rectory garden to thank those who do so much to help. Not just the church folk, but those who care for the buildings—that is their offering to the church community. It has been good to meet together. Some have not been able to come, but they have been invited, they are being considered and not being taken for granted. We have looked at all the meetings—back to that word *communication*—and tried to even them out a little. It's not easy—just the six PCCs meeting five times a year adds up to thirty meetings! We have thought of having joint PCCs to make the load easier for Liz and myself, but we have not got it right yet. When I first came there was a children's group, called Friday Club, meeting once a week on a Friday during term time. This was a time for youngsters to get together, play games, have a Bible story and make different things. However there were sometimes more helpers than children. The helpers were tired and it was decided to stop. Such a decision is always difficult, but sometimes God calls us to stop and rethink. We hold an annual event for children who have been baptised, a teddy bears picnic, and occasional informal 'messy church' events in Woodton village hall. Many children come and share in the Christingle services on Christmas Eve. Liz and I are welcome into the state primary schools in the Group to lead assemblies. This is a wonderful opportunity to get to know the children and support the staff, and to show that vicars are just normal people. I've also learnt to have a prayer or a few words up my sleeve, just in case a teacher comes up and says 'Can you just...?' Children's work is not easy and part of the Christian life is adapting to situations, and being flexible. Who knows where this will take us in the future?

These are three small rural primary schools: two with about thirty-five children and one with about ninety. They are well run by a dedicated group of teachers and support staff. It's rather like having a big family. This was best expressed at a leavers' assembly where some of the parents and the children were in tears about the 'family' breaking up and moving to new places. It's a great joy to be part of this environment. We may not have a Sunday School or Friday Club, but God's love and Word is being shared with a young generation in a different way. Perhaps this is a new approach—the church goes to where the children are. Thinking about it, is that not what Jesus did all those years ago? He went to where the people were.

I put myself forward as a governor to one of the schools. It was not long before I was asked to be chairman, and what a job! It is easy to get caught up with all the red tape to conform to the legal bodies, but it is still a privilege to go into the school, to see the children learning, watching their characters develop, being amazed at their confidence and share in their enthusiasm. To me, that is an important part of Christian ministry.

The churches are open all the time. This is excellent for me as there are no keys to carry round, or lose! It also means that anybody can go in to sit, wonder, pray at any time. About 1000 people each year have written in the visitors' books in our churches, have browsed, sat, prayed or meditated in these buildings. That's a lot of people in this very rural part of Norfolk. It's very important in our busy world to find the time to stand and stare, sit and be. Some don't write in our visitors' books. A group of people have prepared leaflets describing walks around the whole Group and around individual churches, using the many local footpaths, to help people enjoy God's creation in this beautiful area. Once a year Liz and I do the walk around the whole Group, others joining us as and when they can, to see what an excellent job has been done by those preparing the leaflets and to raise some money for Pat Atkinson's Vidiyal Trust. We have recently revamped the prayer boards in each of the churches. Anybody can come and leave a message and those names can be regularly lifted to our Lord in prayer.

So what of the future? God in Christ has been around for a very long time and will continue to be so. However, we live in a transitory period, in which our country is taking a new look at faith and religion. We need to learn to worship in ways that are accessible to all ages, and this is not easy. The farmers—and there are fields all around our churches—depend on the seasons for their livelihood. To a degree our pattern of worship reflects the agricultural economy. In the spring there is a rogation service, as we beat the bounds on the walk round the Group. There is an open-air Lammas Day service when we thank and praise God for the first fruits of the Harvest; in the autumn, the Harvest festival is still an important part of the church year. Perhaps that is something else I have discovered. Farmers might have all this sophisticated machinery, but they are among the few workers these days who are dependent upon the weather. The high-tech cab may tell the driver how much corn is being produced, but if the ground is saturated, there is not a lot that can be done. The seasons are important, a factor forgotten about in the towns.

The Hempnall Group is now present online on its own website and via *A Church Near You*, provided by the Church of England. On our own site we make available details of our services, the church magazine and many other items of interest. I would classify myself as a bit of a technophobe, but realise that modern technology can assist the church in the work we do. Friends from abroad can now gain access to articles, news, and we hope for ever-growing links to other community organisations.

Any worthwhile endeavour will suffer from ongoing difficulties and frustrations. As I write, we are applying for a grant from English Heritage for a new roof at Hardwick. I worry about all the hoops we have to jump through, and the cost, in our efforts to preserve our buildings. It seems that bats are more important than those who worship in our churches! In Hardwick, the fabric of the interior of this ancient building is deteriorating because of the bats and there is nothing that can legally be done about it—procedures seem to be strangling common sense, and are at loggerheads with the down-to-earth approach of the local communities.

We will need new blood in the years to come. Some ask where it will come from. I'm sure that this is a question that has been asked in other generations. Perhaps the answer is to pray, to show the love of God—his compassion, his kindness, his joy—to realise that each of us is special, to make ourselves available, to offer ourselves and encourage each other and to know that the God we worship offers stability, order and peace. These may be small congregations but they are part of a bigger community, a community that has evolved over a great number of years. Most of the people in our church family know each other, they have lived and shared their lives for a good many years, and are involved in many aspects of village life—another difference between urban and rural life. As Carl Dudley says in *Making the Small Church Effective,*

> In a big world, the small church has remained intimate. In a fast world, the small church has remained steady. In an expensive world, the small church has remained plain. In a complex world, the small church has remained simple. In a rational world, the small church has remained the anchor. In an anonymous world the small church calls us by name.

These eight churches have small congregations; they probably always will have, because the villages have small populations. In our frantic world, they offer stability, a wonder, a mystery. Priests over the past 500 years—and all our churches go back that far and further—have been sharing God's Word, presiding at the Lord's Table and singing God's praises in these beautiful buildings. In this part of South Norfolk it is easier to see God's beauty and God's glory than in many other parts of the country.

Michael Kingston

Three and a half years ago, I wondered what I had let myself in for. During that time, I have discovered these communities, brought together some fifty years ago, and still happy to work both separately and together. Characters have come and gone, adaptations have been made for changing times, but God is still very much at work in people's lives and will continue to be as we continue to minister his love to those around us. It is a great honour to be part of the lives of the people in these villages as we get to know and trust each other. I'm very glad I made the decision to come to Hempnall.

Hempnall church

Born in Kent, Michael trained as a chartered surveyor in Nottingham. He worked first in the West End of London, then moved to Norfolk to work across East Anglia. He has been married to Maggie for the past thirty years and they have two girls. Responding to a call to the ministry, Michael, with Maggie and the girls, returned to Nottingham in 1994 for Michael to study at St John's College. He was fortunate enough to return to Norfolk, to serve a curacy in Drayton. He was then appointed as rector to the Plumsteads, and in 2009 came as team rector to the Hempnall Group of Parishes.

The Hempnall Group Now: A Snapshot

Our Reader in training, Jackie Cook, presented a summary of 2012 at the Team Council AGM, and has kindly allowed us to use it to prepare this snapshot of the life of the Group as it approaches its fiftieth anniversary.

The Hempnall Group of Parishes was formed in 1964. Comprising eight churches in six parishes, it became a Team Ministry in 1976 within the diocese of Norwich. The parishes are Bedingham, Fritton and Morningthorpe, Hardwick and Shelton, Hempnall, Topcroft and Woodton.

The clergy team consists of a full time Rector, a part time Vicar and a Reader in training. The life and the work of the group is assisted by a Team Council and a number of Mission Teams dealing with wholeness, learning and growing, families and young people, outreach, finance and social events. The parishes provide local pastoral care. A magazine is delivered to all those living in the Group ten times a year. In addition to weekly services in the parishes, Group services are held monthly and on special occasions during the year.

During 2012, as in other years, we held a Teddy Bears' Picnic (for all children baptised in the Group in the last five years), a Harvest Supper, a Pet Service and a Carol Service. There were Quiet and Away days, and a visit to King's College, Cambridge (one of our patrons), and children's events for both Mothering Sunday and All Saints' tide.

The clergy regularly visit the three primary schools in the Group to take assemblies, and the schools visit the local churches on special occasions.

The Group raised nearly £3,900 in charitable contributions during 2012. This was donated to various organisations, including Christian Aid and the Big C (a Norwich cancer charity), Farm Crisis Network, and Home from Home, a South African Charity providing foster care for vulnerable children. For the third time Liz and Michael did a sponsored walk of about fourteen miles around the Group, visiting the eight churches and raising £360, which was divided between Big C and the Vidiyal Trust, a Christian charity working with vulnerable people in Madurai in South India. The Group has also participated in Operation Christmas Child for the third year, providing over 100 shoeboxes filled with gifts for underprivileged children in Eastern

Europe and Africa. Individual parishes have also raised considerable sums for their own charitable interests.

Visitor numbers continue to rise and it is clear that both tourists and residents appreciate our open-church policy. Our guide books and leaflets have been revised and reprinted. Guides and maps for walks round the churches and the Group are also available in the churches.

Description of the Villages in the Hempnall Group

The eight villages of Bedingham, Fritton, Hardwick, Hempnall, Morningthorpe, Shelton, Topcroft and Woodton are in a quietly rural area of South Norfolk. It has no pretensions to being an area of outstanding beauty, nor is it greatly frequented by tourists. Its charm lies in its ordinariness, its largely unchanging nature, and the fact that it continues to be farmed by local landowners. It lies between the rivers Tas, Waveney and Chet, although only small tributaries flow within the area. In terms of roads, it is bounded by the B1332 linking Norwich to Bungay, the A140 linking Norwich to Diss, and the A143 linking Diss to Beccles—a coherent country district. A walk around the group covers seventeen miles, encircling 13,213 acres.

Our villages offer much of interest. Elizabeth I had connections with Shelton, and is believed to have hidden in the church on one occasion. Lord Nelson's mother grew up in Woodton. The 310th and, later, 93rd Bombardment Groups of the US Air Force were stationed on Hardwick airfield (in Topcroft) during World War Two. Fritton Common is a Site of Special Scientific Interest, and Tyrell's Wood, on the southern edge of the Group, is a noted ancient woodland. Six of our churches have (or have had) round towers.

The population of the villages has remained remarkably stable over the last fifty years, and at the 2001 census numbered approximately 2,800. During this time four public houses, two schools and four shops have closed, but the villages still have three schools, three shops and two pubs. The villages are within comfortable commuting distance of Norwich, but these are certainly not just dormitory villages. Local economic activity naturally includes farms and other agricultural activity, but also a variety of manufacturing and small businesses, many of them home-based. The sense of community is strong, and newcomers are welcomed among the families who have been here for generations. The future looks secure and stable.

Jill Turner and Sarah Patey

A typical month of services in the Group

1st Sunday: Group service
These are held in a different church each month. There could be an invited speaker, and each year there is a pet service, a healing service and an open-air service. The service starts at 10, with refreshment after. This is an important time for the whole group to meet and worship together.

2nd Sunday
8.00 Morningthorpe: Holy Communion, Book of Common Prayer
9.30 Hempnall: Eucharist
9.30 Bedingham or Woodton: Eucharist
11.00 Topcroft: Eucharist
11.00 Shelton or Hardwick: Matins

3rd Sunday
8.00 Topcroft: Eucharist
9.30 Hempnall: United service with Methodists, alternately led by Anglicans and Methodists.
9.30 Bedingham or Woodton: Eucharist
11.00 Shelton or Hardwick: Eucharist

4th Sunday
9.30 Hempnall: Eucharist
9.30 Woodton or Bedingham: Eucharist
11.00 Topcroft: Morning Praise
11.00 Morningthorpe or Fritton: Eucharist

5th Sunday (usually 4 times a year) Group service is held, moving around the group.

Shelton and Fritton are used during the summer months only.

Apart from one monthly BCP service, Eucharistic services are from *Common Worship*. All forthcoming services are listed on the Group website:

www.hempnallgroup.co.uk

Hempnall Group Clergy

Key	**Team Rector**
	Team Vicar
1963–1972	Anthony Lathe
1964–1974	**Peter Bradshaw**
1964–1970	Mark Fitzwilliams
1971–1974	Cedric Bradbury
1974–1981	**Cedric Bradbury**
1974–1979	Michael Woods
1975–1998	Kenneth Gray (retired)
1980–1988	Stuart Nairn
1981–1984	**Jeffery Smith**
1984–1987	Colin Way NSM
1984–1989	**Peter Moss**
1987–1991	Keith James (Curate/Team Vicar)
1991–1996	**Ernest Green**
1994–1996	Dorothy Green (Hon. Curate)
1992–1996	Conal Mahony
1996–2009	**Conal Mahony**
1993–1996	Michael Windridge (Curate)
1997–2001	Frank Howard
2002–	Liz Billett
2009–	**Michael Kingston**